Your Money and

Your Home

# YOUR MONEY AND

# YOUR HOME

## A Step-by-Step Guide to
## Financing or Refinancing
## Your Home

### Sidney Lenz

Griffin Publishing
Glendale, California

Photo on back cover by Richard E. Armstrong

10   9   8   7   6   5   4   3   2   1

ISBN: 1-882-180-00-3

Griffin Publishing
544 West Colorado Street
Glendale, California  91204

Manufactured in the United States of America.

# Preface
*Financing the American Dream*

The dream of most Americans is homeownership. It is also the largest financial investment most of us will make in our lifetime. This book is intended as a guide to unraveling the confusing process of financing that dream. It is full of sound advice on both financing and refinancing a home, with plenty of tips on how to save money. It provides answers to the most commonly asked questions and how to avoid being caught in the scams designed to intercept your monthly payments.

There are numerous worksheets throughout the book; however, a simple calculator and the ability to add, subtract, divide and multiply are all that's needed.

Most Lenders counsel Consumers prior to loan application. Unfortunately, home financing is complicated and becomes increasingly more so each year. Being informed is the key to making the best decision.

Good luck.

# Table of Contents

# I

# BACKGROUND

# 1. Who Are the Players?

### LENDER (MORTGAGE COMPANY)

An institution who loans the money to you to buy or refinance a home.

### REAL ESTATE BROKER OR ASSOCIATE

A professional in the area of buying and selling property.

### APPRAISER

A professional, qualified by education, training and experience to determine the value of real estate.

### CREDIT REPORTING AGENCY

A company who maintains histories of credit records, including public records (for lawsuits, bankruptcies, etc.).

### ESCROW COMPANY

In some western states, Escrow Companies act as a third party to a home purchase. They carry out the wishes of both Buyer and Seller and are responsible for having all documentation executed.

## TITLE COMPANY

A company which issues a Title Insurance Policy on the property. Lenders require that title insurance be issued when making a mortgage loan to insure that they have a valid lien against the property.

## CLOSING AGENT

A company responsible for the proper closing of a mortgage loan. This could be an escrow company, an attorney, or a title insurance agent—depending on local custom.

## SECONDARY MARKET:

FNMA (Fannie Mae)
FHLMC (Freddie Mac)
GNMA (Ginnie Mae)
These Agencies buy loans from Lenders; however, the Lenders continue to collect the payments and, in turn, forward to the Agency.

## HUD

### (Department of Housing and Urban Development)

Insures loans made under FHA programs. HUD and FHA do not loan money for purchase of homes under their regular single family programs. They insure to the Lender making the loan that the Borrower will repay the loan. For this insurance, the Borrower will pay a fee called MIP (Mortgage Insurance Premium).

## VA (VETERANS ADMINISTRATION)

The VA guarantees to the Lender that the veteran borrowing the money will repay it. For this, the veteran will pay a fee to the VA called a Funding Fee.

# 2. The Money Supply for Mortgage Bankers

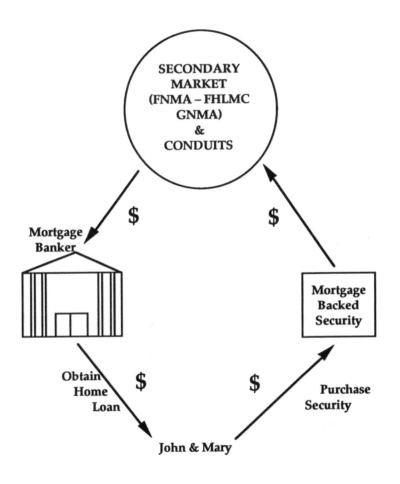

Unlike savings institutions who use savings to fund home loans, Mortgage Bankers do *not* receive

4

deposits but loan money supplied through the secondary market: Fannie Mae (FNMA), Freddie Mac (FHLMC), and Ginnie Mae (GNMA), or through securities backed by mortgages issued internally, or by a conduit—a company who issues securities backed by mortgages purchased from Mortgage Bankers and other Lenders.

# II

# QUALIFICATION

# 3. How Much Can I Borrow Based on the Value of the Home?

Lenders may have different guidelines based on such factors as:

- The loan program
- The property type
- Occupancy
- The purpose of the loan (purchase, refinance balance, refinance to extract equity).

---

Computing the "Loan to Value" ratio (LTV):

| Loan Amount | + | Value of Home | = | LTV |
|---|---|---|---|---|
| $100,000 | + | $125,000 | = | 80% |
| _____ | + | _____ | = | _____ |

---

Generally, these LTV's may apply (remember each Lender may be different).

| | Maximum |
|---|---|
| Purchase a home | 90 to 95% LTV |
| Refinance existing balance | 90% LTV |
| Refinancing existing balance plus cost | 90% LTV |
| Refinance to extract equity | 75% LTV |
| Refinance existing balance on rental property | 70% LTV |

# 4. How Much Can I Borrow Based on My Financial Situation?

**"QUICK REFERENCE"**

Locate in the first line the number closest to your monthly gross income. The column below your income will indicate the loan amount for which you can qualify at each interest rate listed at the left.

## Monthly gross income

| Interest Rate | $2000 | $2500 | $3000 | $3500 | $4000 |
|---|---|---|---|---|---|
| | **Loan amount in thousands of dollars** | | | | |
| 7.0% | 68 | 85 | 101 | 118 | 135 |
| 7.5% | 65 | 81 | 98 | 114 | 130 |
| 8.0% | 63 | 78 | 94 | 110 | 125 |
| 8.5% | 60 | 76 | 91 | 106 | 121 |
| 9.0% | 58 | 73 | 88 | 102 | 117 |
| 9.5% | 56 | 71 | 85 | 99 | 113 |
| 10.0% | 55 | 68 | 82 | 96 | 109 |
| 10.5% | 52 | 66 | 79 | 92 | 105 |
| 11.0% | 50 | 63 | 76 | 88 | 101 |
| 11.5% | 48 | 61 | 73 | 85 | 97 |
| 12.0% | 47 | 59 | 71 | 82 | 94 |

## Monthly gross income

| $4500 | $5000 | $5500 | $6000 | $6500 | $7000 |
|-------|-------|-------|-------|-------|-------|
| **Loan amount in thousands of dollars** | | | | | |
| 152 | 169 | 186 | 203 | 220 | 236 |
| 146 | 163 | 179 | 195 | 211 | 228 |
| 141 | 157 | 172 | 188 | 204 | 219 |
| 136 | 151 | 166 | 181 | 196 | 212 |
| 131 | 146 | 161 | 175 | 190 | 204 |
| 127 | 141 | 155 | 169 | 184 | 198 |
| 123 | 137 | 150 | 164 | 178 | 191 |
| 118 | 131 | 144 | 157 | 170 | 184 |
| 113 | 126 | 139 | 151 | 164 | 176 |
| 109 | 121 | 133 | 145 | 157 | 170 |
| 106 | 118 | 130 | 141 | 153 | 165 |

*Note: Taxes and insurance have been estimated at 0.013% to represent a national average. (Assumes 20% down—30 year term.)*

11

## GETTING SPECIFIC

The first step is to determine the monthly payment for which you can qualify. To do this, you need to calculate two amounts (numbers are rounded).

| Line # | | Your Loan | Example |
|---|---|---|---|
| | **AMOUNT I:** | | |
| A. | The percentage of your monthly income which can be applied to the total house payment – principal, interest, taxes and insurance. | 0.28% | 0.28% |
| B. | Less an adjustment for estimated taxes and insurance. | 0.04% | 0.04% |
| C. | Equals the percentage available for P & I. | 0.24% | 0.24% |
| D. | Gross monthly income (before taxes). Types of income are listed in Chapter 7. | | $6,250. |
| E. | Multiply line D by line C (round). | | $1,500. |

| Line # | | Your Loan | Example |
|--------|--|-----------|---------|
| | **AMOUNT II:** | | |
| F. | Enter your gross monthly income from D. | | $6250. |
| G. | The percentage of your income which can be applied to PITI plus other debts is 36%, less an adjustment for taxes and insurance = 32% available for P & I plus debts. | .32 | .32 |
| H. | Total available for P & I plus debts. Multiply line G x line F. | | $2000. |
| I. | Enter the total amount of your monthly payments to debt (exclude any debt that will be paid off when this loan closes). See Chapter 7 for further information. | | $450. |
| J. | Subtract line I from line H. | | $1550. |
| K. | Enter the lesser of lines E and J. | | $1500. |

You have just calculated the amount of the monthly payment for which you can qualify.

The next step is to determine what loan amount will result in the monthly P & I payment you just calculated. The amount will vary depending on the interest rate and term (number of years) you select. Compare a few options. Select the factor from the table in Appendix B.

| (Rate/Term) | Amount from Line K | | | Loan Amt. |
|---|---|---|---|---|
| (_____) | $_____ | + _____ | = | $_____ |
| (_____) | $_____ | + _____ | = | $_____ |
| (_____) | $_____ | + _____ | = | $_____ |
| (_____) | $_____ | + _____ | = | $_____ |

Example:

| (8%/30 yrs.) | $1500. | + | .00734 | = | $204,350. |
|---|---|---|---|---|---|
| (8%/15 yrs.) | $1500. | + | .00956 | = | $156,900. |
| (7%/15 yrs.) | $1500. | + | .00899 | = | $166,800. |

As you can see, in the example, the longer term results in the higher loan amount—a difference of $47,450. While a lower rate with equal terms results in a lower loan amount.

# III

# PROBLEMS

# 5. Credit Problems

*"I've had credit problems — can I qualify for a home loan?"*

Lenders look at your attitude toward meeting your obligations.

## ATTITUDE IS THE KEY

Examples:

• *You had a period of time, 12 to 18 months ago, where you paid most of your obligations 30 to 60 days late. Since then you have paid on a timely basis.*

Your Lender will want to know why the late payments occurred. However, since you gained control of the situation and have since been making your payments on time, with an acceptable explanation, this situation will probably not affect your application for a home loan.

• *You filed bankruptcy 2 years ago.*

Lenders will look for the bankruptcy to have been discharged at least 2 years ago, and credit re-established since that time. The Lender will also evaluate the reason for the bankruptcy.

• *You have outstanding liens or judgments.*

The Lender will evaluate the *reason* the lien or judgment was filed. Also, these items will have to be satisfied before loan closing.

16

# 6. I Don't Have Enough Cash! What Can I Do?

• **Borrow with a secured loan.** Although borrowing on an unsecured basis to meet the needs of the cash investment in a real estate financing transaction is not acceptable to Lenders, it is indeed acceptable to borrow on a secured loan. Remember, the monthly payment, if any, will be considered when calculating your income qualification ratios. Here are a couple of suggestions:

- A loan secured by your life insurance
- A loan from your 401K deposits

• **Lease with an option to buy** and pay more. This is tricky and requires patience, but if you've had trouble saving enough money, perhaps this is the way.

You'll need to find a property and have the cooperation of the owner/seller. The **rent/lease** payment made to the owner must be a fair market rent. Contact two appraisers in your area and obtain their assessment—**in writing**—of the fair rental value. This must be equal to or less than the rent/lease payment to the owner. Establish a dollar amount over and above the rent/lease payment to be applied toward the purchase price. The lease agreement must state that this amount will be applied toward the down payment if the option is exercised.

Example:

| | |
|---|---|
| Fair market rent | $1500. per month |
| Rent paid | $1700. per month |
| Additional amount paid toward purchase | $200. per month |
| Amount applied toward purchase after 12 months | $2,400. ($200 x 12) |

• **Gifts**. If you are lucky enough to have a family member who will give you money to help with the purchase of a home, this is generally acceptable for a portion of the down payment with the following conditions:

> • The funds must be a gift with no repayment required or intended.
> • At least 5% of the funds required must be from your own resources with amounts over 5% from a gift.

• **Use of early first payment** to reduce money needed at closing (See Chapter 33, "How to Reduce Cash Required at Closing").

If you plan to use any of these methods, discuss the plan with the Lender. Ask the Lender:

| What are the requirements for the method I plan to use? |
|---|
| Loan |
| Lease |
| Gift |
| Early First Payment |

# IV

# INCOME/DEBTS

# 7. Income and Debts

## INCOME

The following is a partial list of the types of income which may be used in calculating affordability:

- Wages, salaries, tips, bonuses, etc.
- Self-employed—business income less expenses plus depreciation (See Chapter 8)
- Social Security income
- Retirement pay
- Veterans compensation or pensions
- Child support or alimony which will continue for at least 5 years
- Pension
- Military retirement
- Paid up annuities
- Estates or trusts
- Disability
- National guard or reserve pay
- Mortgages receivable
- Royalties
- Real estate rents, less cost, less vacancy factor (See Chapter 9)
- Military allowances
- Other permanent cash income not included elsewhere

Temporary or non cash income is not considered in calculating the monthly payment which you can afford, but may be used to offset short term debt or as a compensating factor. Therefore it should be reported to the Lender.

Examples:

- Federal or State Supplemental Security Income (SSI)
- State unemployment compensation
- Supplemental unemployment compensation
- Other supplemental unemployment compensation
- Workers compensation
- State, employer or union temporary sickness or disability benefits
- Aid to families with dependent children (AFDC)
- General assistance or general relief
- Refugee assistance
- Foster child care payments
- Welfare
- GI Bill or other VA educational assistance
- Relatives or friends
- Roomers or boarders
- Incidental or casual earnings

## DEBT

To arrive at your monthly payment to debt when calculating the homeloan payment for which you can qualify, include all payments to:

- Credit cards
- Automobile loans
- Boat loans
- Bank loans

- Charge accounts
- Personal loans
- Outstanding home mortgages*
- Child support
- Alimony
- All other loans

\* If the mortgage is on real estate owned other than the home to be purchased or refinanced:

The positive or negative cash flow from your tax returns will be considered. Depreciation will be added to your income or subtracted from your loss. (See Chapter 9.)

\* If the mortgage is on the home to be refinanced and it will be paid off with the refinance proceeds, it is **not** considered in the calculation.

# 8. Self-Employed

For mortgage lending purposes, a person is generally considered self-employed if they own 25% or more of a business.

Computing income and the documentation required:

## Sole Proprietor or Partnership

### Income

- Net income from past 2 years' tax returns, plus year to date income
- Plus depreciation
- Averaged for monthly income

*Income not reported to the IRS will not be considered (except current year income).*

### Documentation

- Tax returns for the most recent 2 years—including all schedules (signed)
- Year-to-date profit and loss statement (signed)
- Current balance sheet (signed)

## INCORPORATED

### Income

- Income from W-2 (personal and corporate tax returns must support the W-2 information)

*Income not reported to the IRS will not be considered.*

23

**Documentation**

- Personal tax returns including all schedules and W-2's for the most recent 2 years (signed)
- Corporate tax returns, including all schedules for the past 2 years (signed)
- Current balance sheet (signed)
- The Lender will obtain a business credit report in addition to a personal credit report.

Determine **your** income for mortgage lending purposes:

| | |
|---|---|
| Net Income for most recent year from Tax Return | $_____ |
| Add Depreciation from Tax Return | + $_____ |
| Net Income for prior year from Tax Return | $_____ |
| Add Depreciation from Tax Return | + $_____ |
| Add year to date income _____ (a) months | $_____ |
| TOTAL INCOME | $_____ |

Divide total by 24 plus the number of months added in year to date income above (1) for monthly income which will be used by the Lender.

24 + _____ (a) = _____

Total Income $_____ + _____ = $ _____

Example:

Year to date 5 months (January thru May)

$$24 \times 5 \text{ (a) } = 29$$

Total Income $203,000 ÷ 29 = $7,000.

# 9. Rental Income

When you own property on which you receive rental income, the Lender will consider this income if you are planning to retain ownership.

Here's how to determine the amount:

• Complete the amounts based on your most recent two years tax returns:

| | |
|---|---|
| Year One: income from real estate | $_____ |
| plus depreciation | +_____ |
| Year Two: income from real estate | $_____ |
| plus depreciation | +_____ |
| TOTAL | $_____ |

• Divide the total by 24 to determine the monthly income which the Lender will use.

$$\$_____ \div 24 = \$_____$$

If this is a negative figure, the Lender will consider it as a debt.

Be prepared to provide the Lender with the following documentation:

• Most recent two years tax returns with all schedules (signed)
• Lease(s)

If you have owned the property less than two years, the Lender may consider the income only as a compensating factor; however, any negative cash flow will be considered as a debt.

To estimate the income/debt on property owned for a short period of time:

| | | |
|---|---|---|
| Total income from rent | $_____ | |
| Less monthly payment to P & I | – $_____ | (1) |
| Less monthly payment to taxes | – $_____ | (2) |
| Less monthly payment to insurance | – $_____ | (3) |
| Less vacancy factor | – $_____ | (4) |
| Less homeowners association fee | – $_____ | |
| TOTAL | $_____ | |

(1) Monthly payment to principal and interest—if your payment includes taxes and insurance, enter the total payment and skip (2) and (3).

(2) If your taxes are not included in the monthly payment, divide the annual taxes by 12 and enter result.

(3) If your insurance is not included in the monthly payment, divide the annual insurance premium by 12 and enter the result.

(4) Vacancy factor —Ask your Lender:

| |
|---|
| What vacancy factor will be used in determining my income from Real Estate? _____ % |

Multiply the Total Rental Income by the vacancy factor and enter the result.

Example: $2,000 rent x 5% vacancy factor = $100.

$_____ x _____% = $_____
Rent   Vacancy
Factor

# 10. Calculating Total Income

## WORKSHEET

**Present** monthly base pay
from employment (Borrower 1)                    $_____
            (Borrower 2)                        $_____

**Commission and/or Bonus**
Income
• From last two tax      (1) $_____
  returns                (2) $_____

• Year to date from pay stub    $_____

            TOTAL        $_____

Divide by 24 plus the number
of months used in year to date
(monthly average for 2+ years)  + _____  =  $_____

**Part Time**
If income has been
consistent over at least a 2-year
period—monthly amount                           $_____

**Self-Employed**
See Chapter 8 and
enter monthly total                             $_____

**Rental Income**
See Chapter 9 and
enter monthly total                             $_____
**Other Income**
Income received on a regular

basis over the past 2 years which
will continue for at least 5 years
and can be verified.

| _____ | $_____ |
| _____ | $_____ |
| _____ | $_____ |
| TOTAL | $_____ |

# V

# LOAN TYPES

# 11. Popular Mortgage Types–

## HOW DO I SELECT THE RIGHT ONE FOR ME?

There is no right or wrong mortgage. The selection should be based on your personal preference. The product features listed below should help you make an informed decision.

## FEATURES/ADVANTAGES/DISADVANTAGES

### Fixed Rate

#### Features

- A fixed principal and interest payment is made monthly during the term of the loan.
- Loan is paid in full at the end of the loan term.
- Different terms are available.

#### Advantages

- The monthly principal and interest payment is always known and does not change.
- Amortizes over the life of the loan.
- As interest rates change during the life of the loan, the payment remains the same (an advantage when rates are increasing).

### Disadvantages

- As interest rates change during the life of the loan, the payment remains the same (a disadvantage when rates are decreasing).

## Balloon

### Features

- Monthly principal and interest is based on a 30-year amortization (mortgage term).
- Balance is due at the end of the Balloon period. The most common are 5 years, 7 years or 10 years.

### Advantages

- Usually are available at a lesser price (rate and/or points) than a fixed rate loan.
- If you plan to live in the home for less than the balloon period, this loan offers the advantages of a fixed rate loan at a lower price.

### Disadvantages

- At the end of the balloon period, this loan must be paid off, or refinanced.

## ARM(Adjustable Rate Mortgage)

### Features

- Interest rate adjusts at established intervals, based on established index rate.
- Usually have a cap on the payment increases, both for each adjustment period and for the life of the loan.

- See Chapter 12. Adjustable Rate Mortgages are very complex and the ARM Chapter explains these mortgages in greater detail.

## Advantages

- Lower beginning rate allows you to qualify for a higher loan amount.
- If the index interest rates decrease during the life of the loan, the interest rate on your loan also decreases.
- Many ARM loans may be converted to a fixed rate loan at some period during the life of the loan.
- Often the very low start rate adds up to significant savings during the first two years.
- The "worst case" is always known.

## Disadvantages

- The unknown fluctuations in monthly payments may be unacceptable to you.
- Conversion rate will be slightly higher that the market rate at the time the loan is converted to a fixed rate.

# Buydown

## Features

- The interest rate may be lowered by paying points (see Points—Friend or Foe, Chapter 16) or escrowing Buydown funds.

## Advantages

- Lower monthly payments during the life of the loan is an advantage if you plan to remain in the home a sufficient period of time to recover the cost of the points.

### Disadvantages

- Requires cash up front to pay higher points.

## FHA

### Features

- Insured by the FHA.
- Generally, lower down payment than conventional loans.
- Maximum loan amount is established by FHA and is different for each area.

### Advantages

- Less cash required.

### Disadvantages

- Restricted loan amount.
- Both up front and monthly mortgage insurance premiums required.

## VA

### Features

- For eligible veterans, a no-down-payment loan.
- Maximum loan amount is established by VA; however, it is higher than FHA limits.

### Advantages

- No down payment required on most loans.

### Disadvantages

- None — go for it if you are eligible!

# QUESTIONS TO ASK YOUR LENDER:

**FIXED RATE**

> Are rate/points different
> if the term is different? _____

**BALLOON**

> When is the total amount due? _____
> Are the rate/points different based on
> when the loan is due? _____

**ARM**

> See ARM Chapter 12.

**BUYDOWN**

> If refinancing, can the points
> be financed? _____

**FHA**

> What is the maximum FHA
> loan in my area? $ _____

**VA**

> Am I eligible (based on
> my service record)? _____
> What is the maximum
> VA loan amount? $ _____

# 12. ARM Loans
# (Adjustable Rate Mortgage)

An Adjustable Rate loan is a type of mortgage in which the Interest Rate changes periodically according to a predetermined index.

The following are elements of an ARM loan and what they mean:

•   **INDEX**—The published interest rate on which the rate on your loan is based. A predetermined **Margin** (explained below) is added to the Index when the interest rate is adjusted. The Indices most frequently used are:

> • 1-year Treasury Bill
> • 11th District Cost of Funds

Lenders may not use a rate over which they have any control. See page 40 for the past performance of the popular indices.

•   **MARGIN**—An amount set by the lender which is added to the index to determine the mortgage interest rate.

•   **FULLY INDEXED RATE**—The total of today's Index Rate plus the Margin.

•   **ANNUAL RATE CAP**—The maximum your interest rate can increase at each annual adjustment.

•   **LIFE CAP**—The maximum your interest rate can increase during the life of the loan.

•   **CONVERSION OPTION**—Some ARM loans will allow for conversion to a fixed rate loan (usually during the second to fifth year of the loan). If you exercise this option, you will pay a one-time fee of a few hundred dollars and the rate will be slightly higher than fixed rate loans at the time of conversion. Of course, you can also refinance the loan.

• **NEGATIVE AMORTIZATION**—This means that you are not paying a sufficient amount each month to cover the interest; therefore, the principal balance increases. Very few loans today have this feature, and you probably **don't** want it. Be sure to ask the question.

What does this all mean to you? Let's compare some ARM loan features and some "what ifs":

|                                      | (A)   | (B)   |
|--------------------------------------|-------|-------|
| Today's index                        | 4.5%  | 4.5%  |
| Lenders set margin                    | 2.5%  | 3.0%  |
| Fully indexed rate                    | 7.0%  | 7.5%  |
| Start rate (beginning payment rate)   | 4.5%  | 4.0%  |
| Annual cap                            | 2.0%  | 2.0%  |
| Life cap (6% above start rate)        | 10.5% | 10.0% |

In this case, loan (B) has increased the margin to help offset the risk of the lower start rate.

Is this good or bad?

• Suppose rates remain the same for one year and it is time for the first payment adjustment:

|                                                      | (A)   | (B)   |
|------------------------------------------------------|-------|-------|
| Start rate                                            | 4.5%  | 4.0%  |
| Plus annual cap                                       | 2.0%  | 2.0%  |
| **New rate**                                          | 6.5%  | 6.0%  |
| Fully indexed rate                                    | 7.0%  | 7.5%  |
| New payment (lower of capped rate and fully indexed rate) | 6.5%  | 6.0%  |

Although the margin is higher on loan (B), the new payment is based on the **lesser** of the fully indexed rate or the start rate plus the cap.

In this case, loan (B) has the lower payments for the first 2 years.

- Suppose rates reduce by 1.5% during the first year:

|  | (A) | (B) |
|---|---|---|
| Start rate | 4.5% | 4.0% |
| Plus annual cap | 2.0% | 2.0% |
| **New Rate based on cap** | **6.5%** | **6.0%** |
| Fully indexed rate | 5.5% | 6.0% |
| New payment (lesser of capped rate or fuller indexed rate) | 5.5% | 6.0% |

In this case, loan (A) pays a lower amount in year two—remember loan (B) paid a lower amount in year one.

- Suppose rates increase by 1.5% (to 6%) during the first year:

|  | (A) | (B) |
|---|---|---|
| Start rate | 4.5% | 4.0% |
| Plus annual cap | 2.0% | 2.0% |
| **New Rate** | **6.5%** | **6.0%** |
| Fully indexed rate | 8.5% | 9.0% |
| (Rate 6.0% + margin) |  |  |
| New payment rate | 6.5% | 6.0% |

Loan payments are capped at 6.5% for (A) and 6% for (B); therefore, (B) pays the lower amount for years one and two.

BE AWARE of the differences. There are no right or wrong answers. The performance of an ARM loan depends on the future performance of the interest rate index selected.

It may help to compare "worst case scenarios" which you can do by using the following Worksheet.

## WORST CASE SCENARIO

|  | #1 | #2 | #3 | #4 | Example |
|---|---|---|---|---|---|
| Life Cap |  |  |  |  | +6% |
| Start Rate |  |  |  |  | 4.5% |
| Life Cap + Start Rate |  |  |  |  | 10.5% |
| Annual Cap |  |  |  |  | 2% |
| Start Rate Yr. One Pmt. |  |  |  |  | 4.5% |
| + Annual Cap* Yr. Two Pmt. |  |  |  |  | 6.5% |
| + Annual Cap Yr. Three Pmt. |  |  |  |  | 8.5% |
| + Annual Cap Yr. Four Pmt. |  |  |  |  | 10.5% |
| + Annual Cap |  |  |  |  | NA |
| Remainder of Mortgage: |  |  |  |  | 10.5% |

*Add the annual cap amount only until life cap as in #1 above is reached

When shopping for an ARM loan, compare these features:

| | (1) | (2) | (3) | (4) |
|---|---|---|---|---|
| Lender | | | | |
| Start Rate | | | | |
| Points | | | | |
| Annual Cap | | | | |
| Life Cap | | | | |
| Index | | | | |
| Margin | | | | |
| Fully Indexed Rate | | | | |
| Conversion Option | | | | |
| When | | | | |
| Cost | | | | |
| Negative Amortization yes or no | | | | |
| How has the Index performed over the last 5 years? (See the graph on the following page) | | | | |

INDEX VALUE

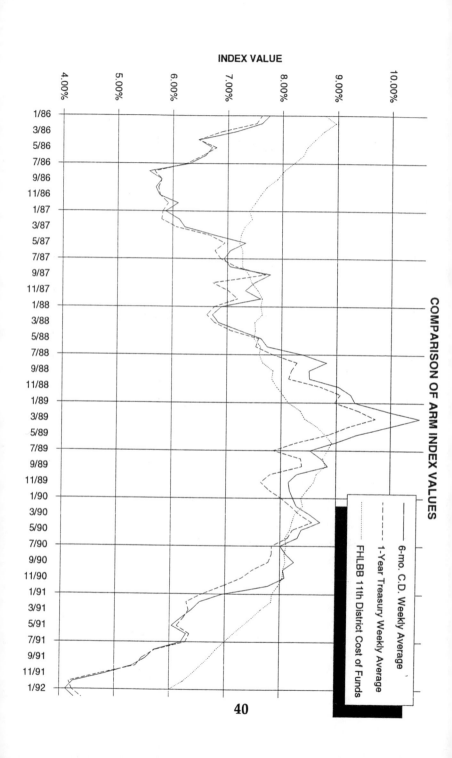

COMPARISON OF ARM INDEX VALUES

— 6-mo. C.D. Weekly Average
---- 1-Year Treasury Weekly Average
········ FHLBB 11th District Cost of Funds

40

# 13. VA Loans and Eligibility

VA rules change from time to time; therefore, be sure to check with your Lender.

---

• Are the October, 1988, eligibility rules still valid? _____

• What is the present maximum VA loan amount? $_____

---

If you meet one of the following military service requirements, you are eligible to apply for a VA loan:

## WARTIME SERVICE

If you served anytime during:

World War II (September 16, 1940 to July 25, 1947)

Korean Conflict (June 27, 1950 to January 31, 1955) or

Viet Nam Era (August 5, 1964 to May 7, 1975)

Desert Storm (August 2, 1990 to a date not yet established by Congress)

You must have served at least 90 days on active duty and have been discharged or released under other than dishonorable conditions. If you served less than 90 days, you may be eligible if discharged because of a service-connected disability.

41

## PEACETIME SERVICE

If your service fell entirely within any one of the following periods:

July 26, 1947 to June 26, 1950

February 1, 1955 to August 4, 1964

May 8, 1975 to September 7, 1980* (if enlisted) or

May 8, 1975 to October 16, 1981* (if officer)

*After these dates: if you were separated from service which began after these dates, you must have—
- completed 24 months of continuous active duty or the full period (at least 181 days) for which you were called or ordered to active duty, and have been discharged or released under circumstances other than dishonorable; or
- completed at least 181 days of active duty with a hardship discharge, a discharge for the convenience of the government, or have been determined to have a compensable service-connected disability, or
- been discharged for a service-connected disability or
- served during "Desert Storm."

You must have served at least 181 days of continuous active duty and have been discharged or released under conditions other than dishonorable. If you served less than 181 days, you may be eligible if discharged because of a service-connected disability.

## ACTIVE DUTY SERVICE PERSONNEL

If you are now on active duty, you are eligible after having served on continuous active status for at least 181 days, regardless of when your service began.

## UNREMARRIED SURVIVING SPOUSES

Unremarried spouses of veterans who were eligible may be eligible to apply for a VA loan.

If you used your eligibility previously, you may be able to use it again:

• If you no longer own the property for which you originally used your eligibility and the loan on that property has been **paid in full (not assumed), or assumed by an eligible Veteran using substitution of entitlement,** you may have your full eligibility amount reinstated.

• If you do not meet the above conditions for reinstatement, but used less than your full eligibility, you may use the **remaining entitlement.**

Ask your Lender:

| What is the maximum VA entitlement amount at this time?  $ |
|---|

Then calculate your maximum loan:

|  |  | Example |
|---|---|---|
| Maximum VA entitlement | $ _____ | $ 46,000 |
| Less Amount previously used | – _____ | – 20,000 |
| Available for use | _____ | $ 26,000 |
| Multiply by 4 | x 4 _____ | x 4 |
| Maximum loan with nothing down | _____ | $104,000 |
| Value of property | _____ | $130,000 |
| Overage (value less maximum loan) | _____ | $ 26,000 |
| Divide by 4 | ÷ 4 _____ | ÷ 4 |
| Down payment required | _____ | $ 6,500 |
| Value | _____ | $130,000 |
| Less down payment = | _____ | $ 6,500 |
| Maximum loan amount | _____ | $123,500 |

## DOCUMENTATION

- Original Certificate of Eligibility
  or
- Proof of Military Service:

    DD 214 if discharged after 1/1/50; or its equivalent
       if  discharged prior to 1/1/50
    Active Duty—Statement of Service from your
       Commanding Officer

## QUALIFICATION

Eligibility for a VA loan means that you are eligible to apply for a VA loan. You still must qualify for the loan.

# 14. Second Mortgages

A Second Mortgage may be a good choice when:

- You have equity in your home you would like to use for other purposes.
- The interest rate on your existing first mortgage is lower than rates presently being offered.

A Second Mortgage is different from a Home Equity Line of Credit. Here's how they compare:

|  | Second | Equity |
|---|---|---|
| • Amortizes over a fixed period of time | yes | no |
| • Interest Rate is fixed for the life of the loan | yes | no |
| • Interest Rate **floats** (usually prime **plus**) | no | yes |
| • Funds disbursed at closing | yes | no |
| • Funds disbursed as needed | no | yes |

Compare your monthly payment when obtaining a second to the option of refinancing.

Example: (numbers rounded)

| | |
|---|---|
| $100,000 | Balance on first mortgage (Original mortgage was $120,000, 30 years at 8% interest) |
| $ 50,000 | Cash needed |
| 9.5% | Refinance Rate |
| 12.0% | Second Mortgage Rate (30-year amortization) |

| | |
|---|---:|
| Payment on first at 8% | $ 881. |
| Payment on $50,000 second at 12% | $ 514. |
| Total | $1395. |
| Refinance $150,000 at 9.5%—30 years | $1261. |

The cost of obtaining the Second and the cost of refinancing must also be considered.

Use the following Worksheet to compare your options.

Ask your Lender:

---

Second Mortgage Interest Rate & Points_____%   _____%

Term over which payment is amortized _____ years

Refinance Interest Rate & Points   _____%   _____%

Term of Refinance   _____ years

What is combined Loan to Value Limit? _____%

---

Placing a Second Mortgage on your property and leaving the existing First Mortgage in place:

## SECOND

- Amount of cash needed                    $ _____  (1)
- Points plus 2% (estimated closing cost)  x _____
- Additional amount needed                 $ _____  (2)
- Add (1) and (2)                          $ _____
- Monthly payment factor                   x _____
  (see Appendix A)
- Monthly payment on new Second            $ _____  (3)
- Monthly payment (P & I) on
  existing first mortgage                  $ _____  (4)
- Total monthly payments (3) + (4)         $ _____  (5)

## REFINANCE

- Balance of existing first mortgage    $ _____    (6)
- Additional cash needed    $ _____    (7)
- Add (6) + (7)    $ _____    (8)
- Points plus 2% (est. closing cost)    x _____
- Additional amount needed    $ _____    (9)
- Total amount needed (8) + (9)    $ _____    (10)
- Monthly payment factor    x _____    (11)
  (see Appendix A)
- Monthly P & I (10) x (11)    $ _____    (12)


Compare line (5) $ _____ with line (12) $ _____


Which results in a lower monthly payment? _____

# VI

# FIRST TIME
# HOMEBUYER

# 15. Help for the First Time Homebuyer

A "first time homebuyer" is usually defined as a person who has not held title to property for at least 3 years. If you owned property but sold it more than 3 years ago, you may be eligible for some special programs.

Although first time homebuyers must come up with a down payment and must qualify for repayment of the loan, in some instances there is help:

• Many State Housing Finance Agencies offer first time homebuyers programs through the Lenders in their state. These programs will generally have lower interest rates and lower down payments than are being offered in the marketplace.

• FNMA/GE Community Homebuyers Program. This first time homebuyer program allows the homebuyer to obtain a loan with 5% down, 2% of which may be a gift from family member or employer.

---

Ask Lenders in your state if special first time homebuyer programs are available? _____
What is the definition of a "first time homebuyer"?
_____

---

• Are you a veteran? The Veterans Administration guarantees loans to Lenders where the veteran pays **no money down**. There is a maximum loan amount for this loan type, however; it is an excellent benefit if you are eligible.

# VII

# TO CONSIDER

# 16. After Tax Cost of Interest

It is interesting to consider your after tax cost of interest when purchasing or refinancing a home. The chart below gives you an estimate of that cost.

Find the interest rate of the loan in the first column–say 9.5%–then refer to that same line under your tax bracket percentage. For the 28% bracket, your interest cost is approximately 6.84%.

| Interest Rate | Tax Bracket: 28% | Tax Bracket: 33% |
|---|---|---|
| 4.0% | 2.88% | 2.68% |
| 4.5% | 3.24% | 3.02% |
| 5.0% | 3.60% | 3.35% |
| 5.5% | 3.96% | 3.69% |
| 6.0% | 4.32% | 4.02% |
| 6.5% | 4.68% | 4.36% |
| 7.0% | 5.04% | 4.69% |
| 7.5% | 5.40% | 5.03% |
| 8.0% | 5.76% | 5.36% |
| 8.5% | 6.12% | 5.70% |
| 9.0% | 6.48% | 6.03% |
| 9.5% | 6.84% | 6.37% |
| 10.0% | 7.20% | 6.70% |
| 10.5% | 7.56% | 7.04% |
| 11.0% | 7.92% | 7.37% |
| 11.5% | 8.28% | 7.71% |
| 12.0% | 8.64% | 8.04% |
| 12.5% | 9.0% | 8.38% |
| 13.0% | 9.36% | 8.71% |
| 13.5% | 9.72% | 9.05% |
| 14.0% | 10.08% | 9.38% |

# 17. Points—Friend or Foe

What is a "Point"? The point is so named because one point is equal to 1% of the loan amount. The use of points allows Lenders to offer an interest rate to you which is lower than the current market interest rate, yet the Lender achieves the same yield.

It's not perfect, but a general rule of thumb is:

1% in points = 1/8% in interest rate.

Therefore, if the present interest rate required in the marketplace is 9%, your options may look like this:

| Interest Rate | + | Points | = | Yield to Lender |
|---|---|---|---|---|
| 9% | + | 0 | = | 9% |
| 8.75% | + | 2% | = | 9% |
| 8.50% | + | 4% | = | 9% |
| 8.25% | + | 6% | = | 9% |

In other words, the Lender is not charging you more by adding points. They are simply achieving the required yield in a combination of rate plus points rather than just rate.

Should you pay points? Maybe! Maybe not!

Ask yourself these questions:

## IF YOU ARE PURCHASING A HOME:

• Will the Seller pay points? _____.
If so, how many? _____.

If the answer is "yes," then you should be shopping for an interest rate which is available for the maximum amount of points the Seller will pay. In the preceeding chart, if the Seller will pay 2 points, you would select the 8.75% rate + 2% in points, not the 9% rate + 0 points.

• Do you want to lower the monthly payment even more, and do you have the cash to pay some additional points and still have enough cash to complete the transaction (down payment, closing cost, moving expenses) and have four month's payments left in reserve? _____. If so, what percentage do you want to pay? _____.

If you pay 2% in the above example where the Seller also pays 2%, then the interest rate for 4% would be selected, 8.5% + 4 points, not 9% + 0 points.

• The effect on monthly payments in the above examples (Based on a $100,000 **30-year fixed** rate loan):

| Interest Rate | Points ($)[1] | P & I Payment[1] | Number of months to recover points paid |
|---|---|---|---|
| 9% | 0 | $805. | 0 (no points paid) |
| 8.75% | $2,000. | $787. | 0 (points paid by seller) |
| 8.50% | $4,000. | $769. | 111 months |
| | | | (Your portion of the points– $2000 ÷ $18 = 111) |

[1] Rounded

In this example, it takes a little over 9 years to recover the points paid by the borrower. Therefore, consider not only whether you have the cash to pay points, but also consider:

• In this example, if you plan to be in the house less than 9 years, you should **not** pay points, but select the lowest rate supported by the points paid only by the Seller. In our example select the 8.75% rate.

If you plan to be in the house more than 9 years, how much will you save? If you plan to remain in the home 30 years, then your savings after recovery of the $2,000 investment would be $4,482 ($18 x 249 = $4,482).

• Is this a fair return on your cash investment? Use the following Worksheet to help you analyze your situation.

# WORKSHEET

## Should I Pay Points When Purchasing or Refinancing a Home?

### Fixed Rate Loan

*This worksheet assumes that you have sufficient cash to pay points.*

- How long do you plan to live in the home?
  # years _____ x 12 = _____ months

- Loan amount $ _____

Ask your Lender:

---

What is the interest rate at no points? _____ %  (A)

What are the lower interest rate options and the points required for those rates?

Rate _____ % points _____ %  (B)

Rate _____ % points _____ %  (C)

---

Now compare the payment amounts.

|  | Option (A) | Option (B) | Option (C) |
|---|---|---|---|
| Loan amount | $ _____ | $ _____ | $ _____ |
| Multiply by P & I | _____ | _____ | _____ |
| Factor from Appendix A | x _____ | x _____ | x _____ |
| P & I payment | $ _____ | $ _____ | $ _____ |

As you can see, the lower the rate, the lower the payment amount. However, the lower rate has a cost (points).

**How long will it take to recover those points?**
(Remember, Option A has no points.)

|  | Option (B) | Option (C) |
|---|---|---|
| • P & I payment | $ _____ | $ _____ |
| • Subtract the P & I payment for the no point Option (A) | – _____ | – _____ |
| • Monthly savings | $ _____ | $ _____ |

## How many points will you pay?

|  | Option (B) | Option (C) |
|---|---|---|
| • Loan amount | $ _____ | $ _____ |
| • Multiply by the points % | x _____% | x _____% |
| • Dollar amount of points | $ _____ | $ _____ |
| • Divide by the monthly savings calculated above | ÷ _____ | ÷ _____ |
| • Number of months to recover points | _____ | _____ |

If the number of months you plan to live in the home exceeds the months to recover, what will your savings be?

|  | Option (B) | Option (C) |
|---|---|---|
| • Interest Rate | _____% | _____% |
| • Number of months you plan to be in the home | _____ | _____ |
| • Less months to recover | – _____ | – _____ |
| • Equals months of savings | _____ | _____ |
| • Multiply the amount of monthly savings | x $ _____ | x $ _____ |
| • Equals total savings | $ _____ | $ _____ |

**What is your decision?**  ❑ Go with 0 point rate
❑ Pay points for lower rate

### If you are refinancing a home:

Let's look at the effect of financing points in order to obtain the lowest P & I payment possible.

In the following example, closing cost (estimated at 2% of the loan amount) plus applicable points have been added to the loan amount and all options are for a **30-year fixed rate loan.**

|  | Present Loan | Option #1 | Option #2 | Option #3 | Option #4 |
|---|---|---|---|---|---|
| Interest Rate | 11% | 9% | 8.75% | 8.50% | 8.25% |
| P & I Pmt. | $1143. | | | | |
| Loan Balance | $115,000. | | | | |
| 2nd Mortgage | $10,000. | | | | |
| P & I | $261. | | | | |
| Total owing | $125,000. | | | | |
| Total P & I | $1,404. | | | | |
| Points | | 0 | 2% | 4% | 6% |
| New Loan Amt. | | $127,550. | $130,150. | $132,800. | $135,500. |
| New P & I | | $1,026. | $1,024. | $1,021. | $1,018. |
| Monthly Savings | | $378. | $380. | $383. | $386. |

As you can see, when comparing 30-year fixed rate loans the best selection is the 0-point option. The payment difference is insignificant when points are financed. Therefore, the 0-point option keeps the total amount owed on the property at a lower amount than the options with points.

As rates and points vary from Lender to Lender, a comparison needs to be made (see Worksheet previously appearing in this chapter). This example only demonstrates the relationship of rates and points in the same program offered by a Lender.

But look what happens when we compare an ARM product with points and closing cost financed.

|  | Present | Option #1 First Year | Option #2 First Year |
|---|---|---|---|
| Interest Rate | 11% | 6.25% | 4.25% |
| P & I Payment | $1145. | | |
| Loan Balance | $115,000. | | |
| Second Mortgage | $10,000. | | |
| P & I | $261. | | |
| Total Owing | $125,000. | | |
| Total P & I | $1404. | | |
| | | | |
| Points | | 0.125% | 3.25% |
| New Loan Amt. | | $127,700. | $129,200. |
| New P & I | | $786. | $636. |
| Monthly Savings-Yr. 1 | | $618. | $768. |

The difference between the points financed in Options #1 and #2 will be recovered in the second year. Also, the lower start rate of 4.25% may result in a lower life cap which is usually based on the start rate plus an added amount.

In this case, it clearly makes sense to select Option #2 and finance the points.

# Are Points
# Tax Deductible?

**YES**, if the following conditions are met:

(IRS Revenue Procedure 92-12)

• The HUD-1 (Closing Statement form) must clearly designate the amounts as points incurred in connection with the loan:

- Loan origination fees
- Loan discount points
- Points

**61**

- The amounts must be calculated as a percentage of the loan amount.
- The amounts must conform to those generally charged in the area.
- The amounts are paid in connection with the purchase of property which will be your principal home.
- The amounts must be paid **directly** by the borrower—not borrowed or received as a gift or sale concession from the seller.
- You must have paid enough cash in the transaction that it would have covered the points. For example, on a loan with nothing down with the Seller paying all the closing cost and points, you would not qualify to deduct points.
- The points must be for the purchase of your primary residence.
- If refinancing your primary residence, the points are deductible in some instances.

(NOTE: Always consult your tax advisor as rules frequently change.)

# 18. To Lock or Not to Lock?

**Lock-in** means that the lender will issue a commitment to you to hold the interest rate and discount points for a certain period of time. Be sure to ask your Lender:

- Do you issue a rate lock? _____
- Is there a charge to me for the rate lock? _____
- If so, how much? _____
- How long will it take to close my loan? _____

When you agree to a rate lock, it is a contract between **you** and the **Lender**. It is a two-way street. If you accept a rate lock, you are expected to close the loan at the terms of your rate lock whether rates go up or down. The Lender also must honor the lock regardless of what happens to rates.

If you choose **not** to lock the rate and points, then your rate and points will be set when your loan is ready to close.

# 19. Term—
# How Do I Select
# the Right One for Me?

Generally, the maximum term to repay a home loan is 30 years, and if you obtain a 30-year loan, you have the option of paying it off in any term you select, simply by increasing your payment.

However, you may get a slightly lower rate by selecting a 15-year term.

Ask your Lender:

> Is there a difference in
> rate and/or points
> if I select a shorter term?

> If so, what term has
> the lowest rate?

Usually, 30, 25 and 20-year terms have the same rate and points. A 15-year term will be slightly lower, but further term reductions do not result in lower rates.

A 30-year term will allow you to qualify for a higher mortgage, but if that is not a factor, then ask about the 15-year term.

The difference in payments (principal and interest) between a 30-year loan and a 15-year loan may surprise you. For example:

$100,000 Loan
9% Interest

|  | 30 yrs. | 15 yrs. | Difference |
|---|---|---|---|
| Monthly P & I: | $804.62 | $1,014.27 | $209.65 |

Although you would pay on the 30-year loan twice as long as the 15-year, the payment is only 26% higher.

Perhaps you're buying the **most** house you can afford, so you need the 30-year payment to qualify for the loan, but you feel that you can afford to repay the loan in 15 years, here's what you can do:

Ask your Lender:

> What would the P & I payment
> be on the loan I am receiving
> if the term was 15 years?

Use this amount to pay additional principal, and the loan will repay in 15 years. In our earlier example, you would make your required payment of $804.62, plus an additional principal payment of $209.65. This would result in the loan paying off in 15 years.

You can use this method with any term—10, 15, 20 or 25 years.

Compare the amount required monthly on the $100,000, 9% loan for early pay off.

| Pay off in: | P & I | Difference |
|---|---|---|
| 30 years | $804.62 | |
| 25 years | $839.20 | $34.58 |
| 20 years | $899.73 | $95.11 |
| 15 years | $1,014.27 | $209.65 |
| 10 years | $1,266.75 | $462.13 |

The best part of planning your own early pay off is that you are not locked into the plan. If your financial circumstances change, you are only *obligated* to pay the amount required by your loan term. In the above example, this would be $804.62.

# VIII

# REFINANCE

# 20. Should I Refinance?

There are many reasons to refinance and each person's situation is different. This section is intended to help you arrive at a good decision.

Place a check mark in the box next to the situation which best describes you:

| Situation | Mortgages to Consider |
|---|---|
| • You have equity in your home and want to extract it for children's college education, paying off existing debts, investing, home improvements, or other reasons. | ❑   30-year Fixed Rate |
| • You have more than one mortgage and would like to combine for a lower payment. | ❑   30-year Fixed Rate<br>ARM<br>Balloon |
| • Your present rate is higher than the current market and you want to refinance to lower your payment and increase monthly cash flow. | ❑   30-year Fixed Rate<br>ARM<br>Balloon |
| • You have an adjustable rate loan and want to lower the payments. | ❑   30-year Fixed Rate<br>ARM<br>Balloon |
| • You want to shorten the remaining term on your home to build equity faster. | ❑   15-year Fixed Rate |

## RULES OF THUMB
(when refinancing to reduce interest rate)

• Generally, you need to retain ownership of your home for 3 years to recuperate the cost of refinancing.

• Interest Rates should be about 2% less than your current rate to make it worthwhile.

# 21. Comparing Types of Mortgages

$100,000 loan (points financed if applicable)
payments rounded

|  | 30-year Fixed Rate | 15-year Fixed Rate | (A) ARM-I (1 yr. T-Bill) $101,400 | (B) ARM-I (1 yr. T-Bill) $103,350 | Balloon 7 yr. |
|---|---|---|---|---|---|
| Interest Rate | 9.25% | 8.75% | 6.25% | 4.25% | 8.75% |
| Points | 0 | 0 | .125% | 3.25 | 0 |
| P & I Yr. 1 | $823 | $999 | $624 | $508 | $787. |
| P & I Yr. 2 | $823 | $999 | $762 | $636 | $787. |
| P & I Yr. 3 | $823 | $999 | $909 | $842 | $787. |
| P & I Yr. 4 | $823 | $999 | $1063 | $969 | $787 |
| P & I Yr. 5 | $823 | $999 | $1063 | $969 | $787. |
| P & I Yr. 6 | $823 | $999 | $1063 | $969 | $787. |
| P & I Yr. 7 | $823 | $999 | $1063 | $969 | $787. |
| And thereafter until paid | $823 | $999 | $1063 | $969 | Balance Due |

(The ARM loans represent the **worst case** possible, both are a 2/6 ARM with a 2% annual cap and a 6% life cap. The full 2% annual cap is applied until the loan reaches it's life cap which is 6% above the start rate.)

Let's compare the total dollars paid on the above loans when held for the number of years indicated:

|  | 5 yrs. | 7 yrs. | 10 yrs. | 15 yrs. | 20 yrs. | 30 yrs. |
|---|---|---|---|---|---|---|
| 30-year Fixed Rate | $49,380 | $69,132 | $98,760 | $148,140 | $197,520 | $296,280 |
| 15-year Fixed Rate | $59,940 | $83,916 | $119,880 | $179,820 | NA | NA |
| (A) ARM-I | $53,052 | $78,564 | $116,838 | $186,618 | $244,398 | $371,958 |
| (B) ARM-I | $47,088 | $70,344 | $105,228 | $163,368 | $221,508 | $337,788 |
| Balloon-7-yr. | $47,220 | $66,108* | NA | NA | NA | NA |

*Balance Due

In analyzing the different product types, remember that the ARM loans represent the **worst case** or highest payments possible over the life of the loan.

• If the loan is held for **5 years** or less: The ARM with the highest points has the least amount of dollars in monthly payments. The difference in points between (A) and (B) is recovered in the 25th payment; therefore, for (A) to be more attractive, the life of the loan would need to be less than 2 years. Note that the payments to the **7-year Balloon** are only slightly higher ($158 total) and require no **up-front points**. Therefore, it is probably a better selection, unless you think the rate will remain low enough for the ARM payments to be lower than the maximum. That, of course, is a judgment call on your part.

• If the loan is held for **7 years:** The **7-year Balloon** has the lowest payback. However, you must be prepared to repay the loan at the end of 7 years (refinancing will have a **cost** associated with it).

• If held for **10 years**: The **30-year fixed rate** has the lowest payback. However, note that the 15-year fixed rate payout after 10 years is $21,120. (21%) higher than the 30-year. At this point there are only 5 years left to pay on the 15-year loan, while 20 years remain on the 30-year loan.

• If held for **15 years**: The lowest payback is still the **30-year fixed rate** loan. Again the difference between the 15- and 30-year payments is $31,680; (21%) with the 15-year now paid in full, while the 30-year still has 15 years to pay.

No one can tell you which loan is best for you. You need to look at all the factors involved and decide which loan best fits your needs.

Let's establish **your** situation in order to compare:

| Line # | | Your Loan | Example |
|---|---|---|---|
| A. | The approximate value of your home today is: (If you do not know, call any real estate professional in your area and ask the selling price for homes of comparable size in your neighborhood.) | $ | $200,000 |
| B. | The approximate amount owed on your first mortgage is: | $ | $115,000 |
| C. | The monthly payment to principal and interest (rounded) is: (If you pay taxes and insurance in your payments, locate the principal and interest amount by looking at the original Note, Mortgage, Deed of Trust or last Account Status from the Lender.) | $ | $1143 |
| D | Current interest rate is: | | 11% |
| E. | Remaining term left to pay (to nearest one year) is: | | 26 yrs. |
| F. | Do you have other mortgages on this property? If so, amount owed on second is: | $ | $10,000 |
| G. | Principal and Interest payment is (rounded): | $ | $261 |
| H. | Interest rate is: | | 15% |
| I. | Remaining term left to pay is: | | 5 yrs. |
| J. | Amount owed on Third Mortgate is: | $ | 0 |

| Line # | Your Loan | Example |
|---|---|---|
| K. Principal and Interest payment (rounded) is: | $ | NA |
| L. Remaining term left to pay is: | | NA |
| M. Total Monthly Obligation on your home is: (Add lines C, G, and K.): | $ | $1404 |

**How much money do you need to achieve your objectives?**

| | Your Loan | Example 1 | Example 2 |
|---|---|---|---|
| Payoff First Mortgage (Line B) | | $115,000 | $115,000 |
| Payoff Second Mortgage (Line F) | | $10,000 | $10,000 |
| Payoff Third Mortgage (Line J) | | 0 | 0 |
| Debt Payoff amount: | | $5,000 | 0 |
| Cash needed for college, investments or other uses: | | $10,000 | 0 |
| Total | | $140,000 | $125,000 |
| Add estimated closing cost.: (Total times .02%) | | $2800 | $2500 |
| N. Total needed excluding points: | | $142,800 | $127,500 |

# 22. Rescission

A "Rescission Period" may apply when you are refinancing your home.

This is a 3-day period in which you may change your mind.

Ask your Lender:

| |
|---|
| Does a Rescission Period<br>apply to the loan I have requested? |

Lenders may calculate the Rescission Period differently. Sundays and National Holidays are never counted; however, Saturdays may or may not be counted.

Ask your Lender:

| |
|---|
| Do Saturdays count in the<br>Rescission Period? |

When will your loan be funded?
Here's how it works:

| SUN | MON | TUE | WED | THR | FRI | SAT |
|---|---|---|---|---|---|---|
| | | | | Closing Docu- ments Signed | 1 | 2 |
| Not Counted | 3 | Loan Funded $ | | | | |

During the 3-day rescission period, you have the right to cancel the loan transaction and have all (if any) funds paid by you refunded — except those used to pay for services such as credit report and appraisal or those disclosed up front as non-refundable. Notice to the Lender must be in *writing* and must be *received* by the lender during the rescission period.

# 23. Beware of Double Interest When Refinancing

If you presently have an FHA mortgage on your home and decide to refinance—timing is very important. Whether you are refinancing to another FHA loan or a conventional loan, the double interest problem may exist.

The **problem** is created by the payoff of the existing FHA loan. On this loan type, interest must be paid through the last day of the month in which the loan is paid off; however, interest on your new loan **begins** the day you receive the loan.

Let's say you are refinancing an FHA loan to a new loan and your loan funding occurs on March 15th. Here's how the interest works:

|  |  | Existing loan (to be paid off) |  | New Loan |  |
|---|---|---|---|---|---|
| Daily interest cost: |  | $30.14 |  | $24.66 |  |
| March | 1 | $30.14 |  |  |  |
|  | 2 | $30.14 |  |  |  |
|  | 3 | $30.14 |  |  |  |
|  | 4 | $30.14 |  |  |  |
|  | 5 | $30.14 |  |  |  |
|  | 6 | $30.14 |  |  |  |
|  | 7 | $30.14 |  |  |  |
|  | 8 | $30.14 |  |  |  |
|  | 9 | $30.14 |  |  |  |
| New loan | 10 | $30.14 |  |  |  |
| closes ☞ | 11 | $30.14 |  |  |  |
|  | 12 | $30.14 |  |  |  |
| Rescission | 13 | $30.14 |  |  |  |
| Period | 14 | $30.14 |  | ← |  |
| New ☞ | 15 | $30.14 |  | $24.66 | New |
| loan funds | 16 | $30.14 |  | $24.66 | Loan |
|  | 17 | $30.14 |  | $24.66 | Clock |
|  | 18 | $30.14 |  | $24.66 | Starts |
|  | 19 | $30.14 |  | $24.66 |  |
|  | 20 | $30.14 |  | $24.66 |  |
|  | 21 | $30.14 |  | $24.66 |  |
|  | 22 | $30.14 |  | $24.66 |  |
|  | 23 | $30.14 |  | $24.66 |  |
|  | 24 | $30.14 |  | $24.66 |  |
|  | 25 | $30.14 |  | $24.66 |  |
|  | 26 | $30.14 |  | $24.66 |  |
|  | 27 | $30.14 |  | $24.66 |  |
|  | 28 | $30.14 |  | $24.66 |  |
|  | 29 | $30.14 |  | $24.66 |  |
|  | 30 | $30.14 |  | $24.66 |  |
|  |  | Clock stops existing loan |  |  |  |

As you can see from this illustration, for 16 days (15th thru the 30th) you pay interest on both loans.

The solution is the timing of the closing and funding of the loan. Let's look at what would happen if this same loan closed on the 26th:

|  |  | Existing loan (to be paid off) | New Loan |
| --- | --- | --- | --- |
| Daily interest cost: |  | $30.14 | $24.66 |
| March | 1 | $30.14 |  |
|  | 2 | $30.14 |  |
|  | 3 | $30.14 |  |
|  | 4 | $30.14 |  |
|  | 5 | $30.14 |  |
|  | 6 | $30.14 |  |
|  | 7 | $30.14 |  |
|  | 8 | $30.14 |  |
|  | 9 | $30.14 |  |
|  | 10 | $30.14 |  |
|  | 11 | $30.14 |  |
|  | 12 | $30.14 |  |
|  | 13 | $30.14 |  |
|  | 14 | $30.14 |  |
|  | 15 | $30.14 |  |
|  | 16 | $30.14 |  |
|  | 17 | $30.14 |  |
|  | 18 | $30.14 |  |
|  | 19 | $30.14 |  |
|  | 20 | $30.14 |  |
|  | 21 | $30.14 |  |
|  | 22 | $30.14 |  |
|  | 23 | $30.14 |  |
|  | 24 | $30.14 |  |
| New loan closes ☛ | 25 | $30.14 |  |
|  | 26 | $30.14 |  |
| Rescission Period | 27 | $30.14 |  |
|  | 28 | $30.14 |  |
|  | 29 | $30.14 |  |
| New loan funds ☛ | 30 | $30.14 Clock stops existing loan | $24.66 ◀— New Loan Clock Starts |

In this example, double interest is limited to one day.

**CAUTION:** If your rate is locked in, be sure you do not delay closing and funding only to lose your rate lock. If the borrower in our example has a rate lock expiring March 20th, he may choose to close on the 16th and fund on the 20th even though he pays 10 days on both loans. This may be preferable to paying a higher rate and/or points if he closes after his rate lock expires. However, if his rate lock does not expire until after March 30th, this strategy is a good one to limit the double interest cost.

When deciding the best day to close, be sure the rescission period is calculated properly. You need sufficient time in your rate lock commitment to **fund** the loan, and not all days count. Read the Chapter on "Rescission" before making your decision.

Ask the Lender who is to be paid off:

---

Will I be required
to pay interest
through the last day of the month
in which the loan is paid off?

---

# IX

# PROPERTY TYPES REQUIRING SPECIAL CONSIDERATION

# 24. Condominium

A Condominium (Condo) is a form of home ownership title. Generally, a homeowner owns the interior space between the floor, ceiling and walls along with a proportionate share of all common areas.

When applying for a loan on a condominium, the Lender will need to look at the entire project. Therefore, be prepared with the following information:

**On an existing project:**

The name, address, phone number, fax number, and contact person of the Homeowners Association.

**On a new project:**

The name, address, phone number and fax number of the Builder.

Refer to the *Insurance—Protecting Your Risk* chapter for special insurance requirements.

The Lender will also request a copy of the Bylaws and Operating Budgets for the past two years as well as a copy of the Master Insurance Policy including Fidelity Bond or E & O insurance. The monthly association fee will be considered as part of your total housing expense.

# 25. PUDs
# (Planned Unit Development)

A Planned Unit Development is a development of single family residences with some common area owned jointly by all homeowners in the development. The common area may be minimal such as landscaping of the entrance and street medians or major such as large landscaped areas, club house, pool, tennis courts, etc. The maintenance fee covers the cost of caring for all of these common areas.

If the property you are purchasing or refinancing is located in a PUD, be prepared to furnish the following information to your Lender:

- Amount of the monthly Association fee.
- Name, address, phone number, FAX number and contact person of the Association.

The monthly Association fee will be considered as part of your total housing expense.

# 26. Property Owned Without Spouse

*"The Federal law gives me the right to own real estate without my husband/wife on the title. The law also gives me the right to have credit (such as a home loan) in my name only."*

*"Then why can a Lender require my husband/wife to sign when I close my loan?"*

The loan will be in your name only and all documents, except one, will be signed by you only.

## HERE'S WHAT, WHERE AND WHY:

**WHAT:** The Mortgage or Deed of Trust (these two documents accomplish the same thing—when recorded, they convey an interest in the property as security for a loan) is the only document which will be signed by a spouse who is not a joint owner of the property. This is not required in all states.

If you are planning to finance property without your husband/wife, ask your Lender:

> Is my husband/wife required to sign the Mortgage or Deed of Trust? _____

**WHERE:** In states with the following laws, a husband/wife will be required to sign:

- Homestead.
- Dower/Curtesy.
- Community Property.

If you are unsure, ask your Lender:

> Does this state have Homestead, Dower/Curtesy
> or Community Property laws? _____

**WHY:** A spouse is asked to sign the Mortgage or Deed of Trust because in each of the instances above, the spouse who is **not** on title may have some rights to the property granted by the law involved.

Therefore, when the spouse signs the Mortgage or Deed of Trust, the Lender may—in the event of a foreclosure—foreclose on the untitled right of the spouse thereby obtaining clear title to the property.

If the spouse does not sign and the Lender forecloses, the Lender might not receive clear title as the spouse would **still** have a claim against the property.

Does this mean the husband/wife is obligated to pay the loan even though they are not a party to the loan? Absolutely not, the spouse signed only for the reason stated in the preceding paragraphs.

# X

# THE PROCESS

# 27. Appraisals – Determining Value

*An appraisal is a determination of value issued by a qualified Appraiser. It is used by Lenders to determine the value of the security.*

**New Construction:** Often a Builder has a new home appraised before it is constructed. This is accomplished by first appraising the land; then the structure is appraised using the plans and specifications.

Typically, inspections are performed at various stages of construction to insure completion in accordance with the plans and specifications.

It is your responsibility to assure yourself that the home is completed to your standards. **The Lender** does not warrant the construction. The Builder **may** issue a Warranty of Construction for one year, and some Builders provide a warranty for up to 10 years from a Warranty Company.

Ask your Builder:

---

Do you provide a Warranty of Construction?

If so, for what period of time? _____

---

**Existing Homes:** The appraiser establishes the value of a home using a replacement cost approach and a market approach.

The **market approach** to value is the one used by Lenders to determine the amount to be loaned against the property. This involves comparing the value of a home with similar homes which have recently sold in the neighborhood.

To be compared, the homes:

- MUST be within a few blocks of the home being appraised, and
- MUST have been sold and closed within the past few months.

In some areas, there are no properties which have sold within the past few months in the immediate neighborhood, in which case the appraiser uses those sales **closest** to the home.

If no homes in the neighborhood have sold recently, then the appraiser uses the **most** recent sales. Property **listed** for sale is not a value indicator and may not be used by the appraiser until sold and **closed.**

The Lender will use the appraisal as a **statement of value only.** The Lender **does not warrant** the condition of the home.

---

It is your responsibility to be sure
the property is in acceptable condition.

---

Some Sellers will provide a one-year warranty from a Homeowner Warranty Company when selling their property. Ask the Seller or real estate professional representing you:

---

Is a Homeowner's Warranty
provided on this home?

---

The value of a home is a constantly changing amount. A home may appreciate or depreciate in value without any changes made to the property. Value indicates an estimate of the amount for which a home could be sold at the present.

# 28. Private Mortgage Insurance— What Is it?

Lenders use Private Mortgage Insurance (PMI) to mitigate their loss in the event of foreclosure. Generally, if the down payment is less than 20%, PMI will be required.

## WHAT DOES THIS MEAN TO YOU?

- Your monthly payment is increased by approximately 1/4 of 1% on a conventional loan to cover the insurance premium.
- The first year's premium must be paid by you when the loan closes. This will be based on the down payment made.

For example (estimates):

- Less than 10% down payment, the PMI premium will be .45 % of the loan amount.
- More than 10% but less than 15%, the premium will be .36 % of the loan amount.
- More than 15% but less than 20%, the premium will be .23 % of the loan amount.
- 20% down will usually not require PMI.

Ask your Lender:

---

- Is PMI required? _____
- How much will I pay at closing? $_____
- How much is the monthly premium? $_____
- Can this ever be discontinued? If so, what are the conditions?_____

---

Often Borrowers overlook the fact that at some point the Private Mortgage Insurance on a conventional loan may be discontinued. Lenders' requirements will differ, but will include items such as:

- Have payments been made on time?
- The LTV (loan to value) ratio at the time of the request.
- Low long has the PMI been in effect?

# 29. What Information Will I Need to Apply for a Loan?

- Social Security numbers of all applicants.
- Complete residence addresses, including zip codes, for the past 2 years.
- Employment history for all applicants for the past 2 years, including:
    - Employer's name, address and phone number.
    - Supervisor's name.
    - Earnings.
    - Employee number if applicable.
- Sources of income other than from employment:
    - Type and amount.
    - Name and address of company who issues payment.
    - How can this be verified?
- Assets:
    - Name, address and account number of all bank accounts.
    - Other than bank accounts, a complete description of asset and how to verify.
- Liabilities:
    - Name, address, account number, balance owed and monthly payment on each liability.

- If refinancing:
    - Name, address, approximate loan balance and monthly payment on each loan on the property.
    - Are junior liens (second or third mortgages, equity lines) to be paid off?
    - Purpose of the refinance.
    - The estimated value of your home.
- If purchasing:
    - The terms of the Purchase Contract:
        - Location of property.
        - Seller's name.
        - Real estate professionals involved.
        - Purchase price.
        - What is the seller paying toward closing cost and points?

# 30. What Documentation Will I Need?

- To verify **income** from salary:
    - Pay stubs for the last 30 days.
    - W-2s for the past 2 years.
- To verify income from a business you own:
    - Income tax returns for the past 2 years with **all schedules.**
    - Year-to-date profit and loss statement.
    - Current balance sheet.
- To verify **income** from other sources:
    - Pensions, etc.
      — Awards letter.
    - Real estate.
      — Tax returns for past 2 years with all schedules.
      — Copy of current leases.
    - Alimony and/or child support.
      — Copy of settlement awarding alimony or child support.
      — Copy of past 12 months canceled checks.
- To verify cash assets:
    - Bank statements for past 3 months.
    - 401Ks statement.
    - Stock broker statement/stock certificates.

# 31. The Loan Process

You've purchased a home or made a decision to refinance, selected a loan and completed an application—what happens next?

**THE PROCESS:**

• An Application is completed by a Lender and with required fees paid by you (usually credit report and appraisal fee).

• The Lender issues to you:

    • Disclosure Statements.
    • Estimate of Closing Cost.

• The Lender will ask you to provide other documentation which you should do as quickly as possible.

• The Lender will request a credit report from a credit reporting Agency. In some cases the Agency will send a copy of the report to you at the same time it is sent to the Lender. If the report shows slow/late payments, outstanding debts not shown on your application, or other credit problems, the lender will require an explanation from you. The Lender will ask you to review the report received or contact the credit reporting Agency for a copy. THE LENDER IS NOT ALLOWED TO DISCLOSE THE INFORMATION ON THIS REPORT TO YOU—IT MUST COME DIRECTLY TO YOU FROM THE CREDIT REPORTING AGENCY.

- The Lender will request an APPRAISAL. Most appraisals are performed by **Independent Appraisers.** The appraisal establishes the market value and condition of the home and provides information concerning the neighborhood and area.
- The Lender may request confirmation of other information in the application.
- The Lender requests a preliminary title report.
- When all the documentation is received, the loan is underwritten (reviewed for approval).
- If PMI (private mortgage insurance) is required, it is requested at this time. An application package is sent to the Mortgage Insurance Company for review and approval.
- An Approval Letter (or Declination Letter) is issued which may have conditions. This should be carefully reviewed by you and items needed to clear any conditions furnished to the Lender as quickly as possible.
- Closing Instructions are issued by the Lender to the Closing Agent or Escrow Company. (If new construction, the home must be complete.)
- You will be contacted to coordinate the signing of closing documents and provide other items such as:

  - Insurance policy or endorsement to the existing policy.
  - Items required to clear title.

- If refinancing, your rescission period begins (3 days).
- After conclusion of rescission period, your loan is funded.

# XI

# THE CLOSING

# 32. Insurance –
# Protecting Your Investment

Now that you are a homeowner, you want to make sure your investment is protected. The lender will also require proof that the security (home) used for the loan is protected.

• Homeowners Insurance—A minimum of fire and extended coverage with special form endorsement must be maintained at all times.

• The Lender must be listed as the mortgagee on all policies until the loan is paid in full.

• If your insurance is not paid by the Lender from a Reserve Account (sometimes called Impound or Escrow Account), you need to renew your policy each year prior to the expiration date and furnish a copy to the Lender. You are responsible for providing acceptable proof of insurance to the Lender without lapse in coverage.

• Ask your Lender:

---

What rating is the insurance company I select
required to have with BEST RATING? _____
(B/III or higher is generally required)

---

• The amount of insurance required is the replacement cost or the value of the improvement on the land.

• Should there be damage to the property resulting in a claim against the insurance, the Lender has the right to control the funds while monitoring repairs to the home.

## CONDOMINIUMS

Fire and hazard policies carried by some condominium projects do not cover the interior walls and built-in appliances. In this case, you will be required to maintain a condominium policy which **does** cover these items.

A copy of the Association's policy will be required by the Lender before your loan closes. A copy of the renewal policy will be required each year.

## FLOOD INSURANCE

The Lender will check your property's location on the Federal Flood Maps. Should the property be in an area deemed to be at risk of flooding, flood insurance will be required.

Adjustments to the Federal Flood Maps may cause a requirement for flood insurance on your home after loan closing. This can occur at any time during the life of the loan.

Changes to the Federal Flood Maps are made by the Federal Government, **not** your Lender.

## OTHER TYPES OF INSURANCE

You may want to consider:

- Mortgage Life
- Mortgage Disability
- Critical Period Life
- Accidental Death

## RESERVE ACCOUNT (ESCROW/IMPOUND)

You may be required to pay, or elect to pay, your insurance through a Reserve Account. Be aware that any increase in the cost of your insurance will increase your monthly payment. For example, let's say you have a Reserve Account and your payment breaks down as follows:

| | |
|---|---|
| $840.00 | Principal & Interest (P & I) |
| 90.00 | Taxes |
| 30.00 | Insurance (30 x 12 = $360 per year) |
| $950.00 | Total payment |

If your premium increases to $420 per year, your payment would change accordingly:

| | |
|---|---|
| $840.00 | P & I |
| 90.00 | Taxes |
| 35.00 | Insurance (35 x 12 = $420) |
| $955.00 | Total payment |

## REFINANCING YOUR PROPERTY

When refinancing your property, the Lender will have a set number of months required of remaining coverage on your insurance policy. Should you have less time, contact your insurance agent and arrange for a renewal.

If you are refinancing with the same Lender, that Lender will already be listed as the mortgagee on the policy. If you are refinancing with a new Lender, you will need to request an endorsement, listing the new Lender as the mortgagee.

Ask your Lender:

> What is the wording required for the
> insurance mortgagee clause?

Refer to the Reserve (Impound/Escrow) Account chapter.

# 33. Real Estate Taxes

Timely payment of real estate taxes protects the title to your property.

The Lender may require, or you may elect, to pay your taxes through a Reserve Account. Refer to the "Reserve (Impound/Escrow) Account" chapter.

When purchasing a home, you will be responsible for the taxes beginning on the day you take title to the property.

To illustrate how this works, let's look at an example:

Taxes last paid 10/31/91    $1200.
Taxes next due 10/31/92    $1200.

Loan closes 6/16/92

Seller share
of the taxes 11/1/91 thru 6/15/92
= 7.5 months @ $100 per month    $ 750.

At closing, the Seller credits this amount to the Buyer; therefore, when the taxes are next due:

Taxes due 10/31/92    $1200.
- Seller credited to Buyer at loan closing:    $ 750.
- Balance from Buyer's resources:    $ 450.

The Buyer is responsible from the day he takes title—in this example, for the period 6/16/92 through 10/31/92 (4.5 months).

If the Buyer has a reserve account, the $750 from the Seller will be paid into this account. If not, it is credited to the Borrower at closing (i.e., Seller pays to Buyer at closing which reduces the amount the Buyer owes the Seller).

Any increase in taxes will increase the monthly payment if taxes are paid through a Reserve Account with the Lender.

For example:

| | |
|---|---|
| $ 900.00 | Principal and Interest (P & I) |
| $ 100.00 | Taxes (12 x 100 = $1200 per year) |
| $ 30.00 | Insurance |
| $1,030.00 | Total payment |

If the taxes increase to $1500 per year, the payment would change accordingly:

| | |
|---|---|
| $ 900.00 | P & I |
| $ 125.00 | Taxes (12 x 125 = $1500 per year) |
| $ 30.00 | Insurance |
| $1,055.00 | Total payment |

Supplemental tax bills are usually not paid by the Lender (even if there is a Reserve Account). These bills should be paid promptly by you. The Lender bases the reserve amount collected on the regular tax billing amount; therefore, there will not be sufficient funds in the account to pay supplemental bills.

Taxes due within 60 days after loan closing will be required to be paid at closing.

Sometimes a taxing authority will send a regular tax bill to the Homeowner even if a Reserve Account has been established. Should this happen, write your loan number on the tax bill and immediately forward to your Lender.

*Remember, it is your responsibility to see that all taxes are paid before they become delinquent unless you have a Reserve Account with your Lender.*

# 34. Reserve Accounts

**(Impound/Escrow)**

A Reserve Account is an account held in trust for you by the Lender for payment of such items as:

- Taxes.
- Hazard Insurance.
- Flood Insurance.
- Private Mortgage Insurance (PMI).

Reserve Accounts are required on many loans—all FHA and VA loans and Conventional loans over a specific loan to value ratio defined by the Lender. Even if not required, you may elect to have a Reserve Account to avoid large lump sum payments to Taxing Authorities and Insurance Companies.

Ask your Lender:

---

Is a Reserve Account
required on this loan?_____

---

If not, may I establish
a Reserve Account if
I choose to do so?

---

# HERE'S HOW THE ACCOUNT WORKS —

An initial deposit is made into the account at loan closing. Deposited is the Seller's share of the Real Estate Taxes and, usually 2-month's share of all Reserve Items. This 2-month deposit ensures that the Lender will have the money to pay all taxes and insurance when due.

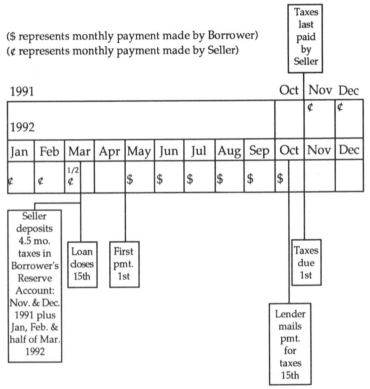

($ represents monthly payment made by Borrower)
(¢ represents monthly payment made by Seller)

In this example, if the Borrower did not deposit 2 months of taxes in the Reserve Account when the loan closed, the Lender would not have sufficient funds on October 15th to pay the taxes.

108

| Count the ¢: | 4.5 | |
|---|---|---|
| And the $: | 6.0 | |
| Total: | 10.5 | months in the account |
| | | |
| Add at closing | 2.0 | |
| Total: | 12.5 | adequate to pay the taxes in a timely manner |

All reserve items work this way.

To understand the amount needed to establish a reserve account for your loan, ask your Lender:

| | Required on my loan? | # Months to establish Reserve Account: |
|---|---|---|
| Taxes | yes | _____ months |
| Homeowners Insurance | yes | _____ months |
| Mortgage Insurance | | _____ months |

Also ask:

Is an additional amount added to tax reserve amount each month to cover tax increases? _____
If so, how much? _____%

Areas may have any number of taxing authorities from one up to five or six.

What happens if your account has too much money, or not enough money —

## TOO MUCH

Once a year, your Lender will issue a Reserve Account Analysis. If there is an overage in the account, the Lender will give you the following options:

- Apply towards the next payment(s) due, or
- Receive a refund.

## NOT ENOUGH

Generally, the Lender will pay the amount due (advancing the funds required) and contact you for repayment. Again, options may apply:

- Repay in one lump sum, **or**
- Repay in 12 equal installments along with your monthly payments.

*The following Worksheet will assist you in determining the amount needed to establish a reserve account.*

# RESERVE ACCOUNT WORKSHEET

| TAXES | Annual | | Monthly | | Addn. Amt. Required for Increase | | Total Monthly | # mo. Req'ed | | Total Reserve |
|---|---|---|---|---|---|---|---|---|---|---|
| _____ | $_____ | +12 | $_____ | + | $_____ | = | $_____ | x_____ | = | $_____ |
| _____ | $_____ | +12 | $_____ | + | $_____ | = | $_____ | x_____ | = | $_____ |
| _____ | $_____ | +12 | $_____ | + | $_____ | = | $_____ | x_____ | = | $_____ |

## INSURANCE (ANNUAL)

$_____ +12 $_____             x_____ = $_____

## MORTGAGE INSURANCE (MONTHLY)

$_____             x_____ = $_____

## OTHER

$_____ +12 $_____             x_____ = $_____
$_____ +12 $_____             x_____ = $_____

TOTAL AMOUNT REQUIRED TO ESTABLISH
A RESERVE ACCOUNT             $_____

## REFINANCING

**With the same Lender**—The Reserve Account may be transferred from the old loan to the new loan with any required adjustments being made.

**With a new Lender**—The Lender being paid off usually refunds the Reserve Account balance to you after about 60 days. This gives the Lender some comfort that the last monthly payment they received from you is a good one.

This delay may cause a hardship for you if you are required to establish a new Reserve Account with the new Lender.

If you know this is going to happen, follow this strategy:

- Once you apply for a refinance, make the payments due during the process by some form of guaranteed payment such as a Cashier's Check.

- Insist that your Lender give you credit for your Reserve Account balance on the payoff statement or refund to you immediately. If your last payment was made with guaranteed funds, they have no reason to refuse this request.

# 35. Closing Cost

Closing Cost vary from area to area and Lender to Lender; therefore, it is important that you confirm the cost for your specific transaction.

Here are some of the common costs:

## SETTLEMENT CHARGES

- **Real Estate Broker Commission**—negotiated by you with your Real Estate Broker or Agent.

## ITEMS PAYABLE IN CONNECTION WITH LOAN

- **Loan Origination Fee or Loan Procession Fee**—set by the Lender and covers the cost of processing the loan.
- **Loan Discount**—set by the Lender. For more information, see the chapter entitled "Points—Friend or Foe."
- **Appraisal Fee**—the fee paid to an Appraiser to appraise the property.
- **Credit Report Fee**—the fee paid to a Credit Reporting Agency to provide a credit report to the Lender.
- **Inspection Fee**—This fee covers the cost of any inspections required on the property, usually connected with new construction.

# ITEMS REQUIRED BY LENDER TO BE PAID IN ADVANCE

- **Interest**—the amount of interest due on the loan prior to the interest paid in the first payment—see Chapter 36.
- **Mortgage Insurance Premium**—see chapter 28, "Private Mortgage Insurance—What Is It?"
- **Hazard Insurance Premium**—the amount needed to pay the premium for the required hazard insurance policy.
- **Reserves Deposited with the Lender**—see chapter 34, entitled "Reserve Accounts."

## TITLE CHARGES

- **Settlement or Closing Fee**—the fee paid to the Closing Agent to handle the loan closing.
  Cost involved with issuance of Title Insurance:

  - Abstract or Title Search.
  - Title Examination.
  - Title Insurance Binder.
  - Title Insurance/Lender's Coverage.

- **Document Preparation Fee**—The fee for preparing the Security Instruments on the loan.
- **Attorney's Fees** (if an attorney is involved)—the fee for his/her services.
- **Owner's Coverage**—optional Title Insurance Coverage for you.

## GOVERNMENT RECORDING AND TRANSFER

### CHARGES

- **Recording fees/City/County Tax/ Stamps/ Deed/ State Tax/ Stamps**—fees charged by the local, state and/or county.

# ADDITIONAL SETTLEMENT CHARGES

- **Survey**—the cost of surveying the property to establish items such as actual lot size, easements, etc.

- **Pest Inspection**—the cost of inspecting the property for infestation, usually required when the appraiser observes and reports evidence of possible infestation.

- **Tax Service Fee**—cost of services to ensure that taxes are paid in a timely manner to protect the title to the property.

- **Flood Check Fee**—the cost of reviewing the Federal flood maps to determine if the property is in a flood area.

# Closing Cost Worksheet

On most loans, the Lender will provide a Good Faith Estimate to you covering all the costs. However, if you wish to prepare your own estimate prior to applying for a loan, use this Worksheet. (Obtain the information from the Lender when "shopping.")

| | |
|---|---|
| Real Estate Commission | |
| (N/A if refinancing) | $ _____ |
| Loan Origination Fee | $ _____ |
| Loan Discount | $ _____ |
| Appraisal Fee | $ _____ |
| | |
| Credit Report | $ _____ |
| Lender's Inspection Fee | $ _____ |
| Settlement or Closing Fee | $ _____ |
| Abstract or Title Search | $ _____ |
| | |
| Title Examination | $ _____ |
| Title Insurance Binder | $ _____ |
| Document Preparation | $ _____ |
| Notary Fees | $ _____ |
| | |
| Attorney's Fee | $ _____ |
| Title Insurance | $ _____ |
| Lender's Coverage | $ _____ |
| Owner's Coverage | $ _____ |
| | |
| Recording Fees | $ _____ |
| City/County Tax/Stamps | $ _____ |
| State Tax/Stamps | $ _____ |
| Survey | $ _____ |
| | |
| Pest Inspection | $ _____ |
| Tax Service Fee | $ _____ |
| Flood Check Fee | $ _____ |
| Warehouse Fee | $ _____ |
| Tax Service Fee | $ _____ |
| Flood Check Fee | $ _____ |
| Other | $ _____ |
| | $ _____ |
| | $ _____ |

- **Total Closing Cost.** $ _____ (1)

- **Prepaid Items:**
  Mortgage Insurance Premium. $ _____
  Hazard Insurance Premium. $ _____
  Prepaid Interest. $ _____
- **Total Prepaid Items.** $ _____ (2)

- **Reserve Account**
  Enter the total from the
  Worksheet in the
  "Reserve Account" chapter. $ _____ (3)

- **Additional Down Payment Due.** $ _____ (4)

- **Total cash due at Closing**
  (Total of items (1), (2), (3) and (4) above.) $ _____

- **If refinancing:**

  (1) may be financed or paid in cash;

  (2) and (3) cannot be financed and
  must be paid in cash.

# 36. How to Reduce Cash Required at Closing

Use of an early first payment does not reduce the amount you ultimately pay; however, it **does** reduce the actual cash you need at closing.

Ask your Lender:

> Is an early payment with an interest credit option available to me? _____
>
> If so, are there limits? (Cut off for the last day in the month I can close using this option.)_____

Here's how interest due is determined when you close a home loan:

Interest is paid in arrears; therefore, when you make your payment on June 1, you are paying the May interest. If you close on April 15 with a June 1 payment, using the regular method, the April interest (15th through 30th) will be due at closing and the first payment will be due June 1 (1st day of second month after closing).

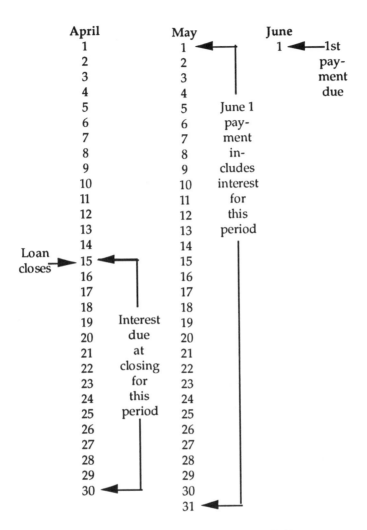

In this example, to determine the dollar amount for the 16 days in April (15 through 30), first calculate the **daily** or per diem interest.

|  | Your Loan: | Example: |
|---|---|---|
| Loan amount | $ _____ | $120,000. |
| Multiply by Interest Rate | x _____ % | x .09% |
| Total | $ _____ | $ 10,800. |
| Divide by 365 | ÷ 365 = | ÷ 365 = |
| Daily (per diem) Interest | $ _____ | $ 29.59 |
| Multiply by number of days to be paid | x _____ | x 16 |
| Amount you **pay** closing | $ _____ | $ 473.44 |

Now let's look at this same example using the Early First Payment method to see how it can reduce the cash you need at closing:

**Early First Payment method:** closing in April, first payment May 1 (1st day of first month after closing).

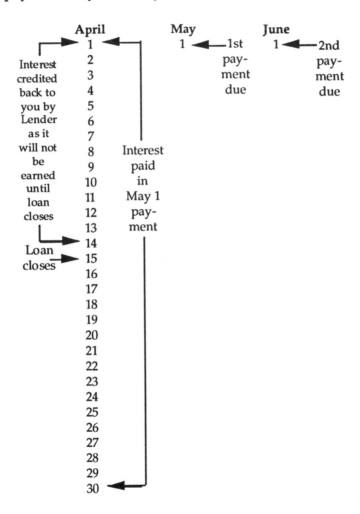

In this example, when the early first payment is due, it will include interest not earned by the Lender; therefore, the Lender *credits* this amount to you in advance.

|  | Your Loan: | Example: |
|---|---|---|
| Loan amount | $ _____ | $120,000. |
| Multiply by interest rate | x _____% | x .09% |
| Total | $ _____ | $ 10,000. |
| Divide by 365 | ÷ 365 = | ÷ 365 = |
| Daily (per diem) interest | $ _____ | $ 29.59 |
| Multiply by number of days interest is unearned | x _____ | x 14 |
| Amount due to you at closing | $ _____ | $ 414.26 |

To compare how these two methods effect the cash you need at closing:

Example:

| | Your Loan | Regular 1st payment | Early 1st payment |
|---|---|---|---|
| Balance of down payment due (NA or refinance) | $_____ | $1,000. | $1,000. |
| Closing cost | $_____ | $3,000. | $3,000. |
| Pre-paids (excluding pre-paid interest) | $_____ | $ 500. | $ 500. |
| Pre-paid interest | $_____ | $ 473. | $ (414.) |
| Total cash you need | $_____ | $4,973. | $4,086. |
| DIFFERENCE in the amount of cash required at closing | | $ 887. less with early first payment | |

It is important to note that this method does not ultimately save you money. Regardless of when the first payment is due, you will pay interest from the day of loan closing. However, what the Early Payment/Interest Credit Method does is reduce the amount of cash you need on the day the loan closes. Be prepared, however, to make the first payment in less than one month.

# XII

# AFTER CLOSING

# 37. One Extra Payment a Year

## HOW CAN YOU PAY OFF A 30-YEAR LOAN IN 21 YEARS AND 6 MONTHS?

Simply pay one additional P & I (principal and interest) payment per year, all of which is applied to principal.

> Pay this amount extra each month:
> P & I Payment $ _____ ÷ 12 = $ _____

To determine the interest saved by following this method, calculate the total amount to be paid on the loan.

- P & I Payment    $ _____
  Multiply    x 360
  Total    $ _____
  (A)

- P & I Payment
       plus 1/12    $ _____
  Multiply    x 258
  Total    $ _____
  (B)

- To Determine Interest Savings:
  Subtract (B) from (A) =    $ _____

Let's look at the effect of an extra payment each year on this loan:

$100,000
30-year Fixed Rate
9.5% Interest

P & I Payment $ <u>891.69</u>  ÷ 12 = $ <u>74.31</u>

| | | |
|---|---|---|
| • P & I Payment | $ <u>891.69</u> | |
| Multiply | x <u>360</u> | |
| Total Payments | | $ <u>321,008.</u>  (A) |
| | | |
| • P & I Payment | | |
| plus 1/12 | $ <u>966</u> | |
| Multiply | x <u>258</u> | |
| Total Payments | | $ <u>249,228.</u>  (B) |
| | | |
| • Interest Savings | | $ <u>71,780.</u> |
| (Subtract (B) from (A)) | | |

The extra $ <u>74.31</u>  per month payment would save $ <u>71,780.</u> in interest over the life of the loan.

If you plan to pre-pay principal, be sure to indicate each month on the payment coupon the amount of the additional payment. The sample coupon below shows how this should be done.

| LOAN NUMBER | PAYMENT DUE - "ON OR BEFORE" |
|---|---|
| 737725  25 | $966.00   JUN 1, 90 |
| | "LATE" PAYMENT - RECEIVED AFTER |
| **MORTGAGE** | $1006.73   JUN 16, 90 |
| Funding Corporation | ADDITIONAL AMOUNT REMITTED: |
| *No checks! No coupons! No postage costs! It is convenient and free! Sign up for automatic payments from your checking account now.* | Principal: **$80.00** Escrow: _____ Other: _____ Total: _____ |
| JANE WEATHER 123 HALE STREET LOS ANGELES,        CA  91201 | PLEASE DO NOT STAPLE CHECK TO COUPON |
| 737725 4000 3 3900  389202 | |

# 38. Automatic Mortgage Payments

To make your mortgage payment each month without writing a check, ask your Lender:

> Can I use Automatic Mortgage Payments?_____
> Can I select the day of the month?_____

The Lender will automatically deduct your mortgage payment each month directly from your checking account. In most cases, you may select the day of the month on which this happens.

**No forgetting! No inadvertent late payments because of failed memory or failed postal service! No worry when you are travelling!**

# 39. My Loan Has Been Sold to Another Lender—Why?

*What did I do wrong?*

*Nothing!*

From time to time, Lenders will sell the Loan Servicing (collection of payments, etc.) on some loans. This has nothing to do with you, it is a business decision made for a variety of reasons.

In this event, you will receive notification from the Lender to whom you currently make your payment, that effective some date in the future your payments are to be made to another Lender. You will also receive notification from the new Lender along with instructions on where to make your payments.

If you do not receive clear instructions, telephone the new Lender to avoid having your payment go astray.

If you do not receive notification from your present Lender, **DO NOT** forward payment anywhere else until you have spoken to your present Lender and confirmed that the payment should indeed go to another Lender.

If you presently have a Reserve Account, it will be transferred to the new Lender.

# 40. Be on the Lookout

- **Improper Collection of Payments:** If you receive notification from a company that they have purchased your loan and you should begin sending payments to them — **DON'T DO IT** unless you have been instructed to do so by your current Lender.

Payments have been improperly diverted in this way.

Transfer of loans is a common business practice, but be sure it is a legitimate transfer.

- **Payment Interception:** It is possible that checks sent through the mail may be improperly intercepted. If you receive a notice from your Lender that a payment has not been received and you know sufficient time has passed for receipt of the check, do **not** assume the mail is slow and ignore the notice. **Telephone your Lender** immediately.

- **Payments Made to a Third Party:** If you make your mortgage payment to a third party who then remits to the Lender, be aware that you are *obligated* to the Lender, even if you made the payment and the third party failed to remit.

There are some legitimate companies that provide such services as:

- Collecting one-half of your payment bi-weekly, remitting to the Lender monthly and accumulating the excess to make one extra payment a year.

- A Shared Investment where you pay a higher amount to a third party than the amount due on the loan. The third party remits the amount due to the Lender and keeps the remainder.

Assure yourself before entering into a Third Party arrangement that the company is legitimate and financially sound. Even then, if for any reason (such as bankruptcy) they fail to pay the Lender, *you* are still on the hook for any payments not received by the Lender, although you may have paid the Third Party.

• **Two Notes:** If you sign two Notes, you may be asking for trouble. Each Note may be sold, and you may owe two people or companies for the same loan.

# XIII

# APPENDIX

# Appendix A

## PRINCIPAL & INTEREST PAYMENT FACTORS

| Interest Rate | 30-Year Loan | 15-Year Loan |
|---|---|---|
| 7.0% | .00666 | .00899 |
| 7.5% | .00700 | .00928 |
| 8.0% | .00734 | .00956 |
| 8.5% | .00769 | .00985 |
| 9.0% | .00805 | .001015 |
| 9.5% | .00841 | .001045 |
| 10.0% | .00878 | .001075 |
| 10.5% | .00915 | .001106 |
| 11.0% | .00953 | .001137 |
| 11.5% | .00991 | .001169 |
| 12.0% | .001029 | .001201 |
| 12.5% | .001068 | .001233 |
| 13.0% | .001107 | .001266 |
| 13.5% | .001146 | .001299 |

*Multiply the loan amount by the appropriate factor.*

## Example:

$175,000, 30-year loan at 7% interest
$175,000 x .00666 = $1165.50 monthly payment.

# Appendix B

## ABSTRACT OF TITLE

A written history of the property title from the original source of title to the present.

## ACCRUED INTEREST

The amount of interest due since interest was last paid.

## ADJUSTABLE RATE MORTGAGE LOAN (ARM)

A type of mortgage in which the interest rate changes periodically according to a predetermined index.

## AGREEMENT FOR SALE

A written document by which a Buyer agrees to buy and a Seller agrees to sell real property.

## AMORTIZATION

Repayment of a debt in equal installments resulting in retirement of the debt — rather than interest only payments.

## AMORTIZATION SCHEDULE

A schedule of each payment due on a mortgage loan showing the amount applied to principal, the amount applied to interest and the remaining principal balance due.

## ANNUAL PERCENTAGE RATE (APR)

A rate which represents the total cost of the loan, including finance charges.

## APPLICATION

The form used and the process of applying for a mortgage loan.

## APPRAISAL

A report by a qualified person setting forth an opinion of value.

## APPRECIATION

An increase in value of real estate.

## BALANCE SHEET

A statement of assets, liabilities and net worth.

## BALLOON MORTGAGE

A mortgage with monthly payments due for a certain period of time at the end of which the remaining balance is due.

## CAP

A limitation on the interest rate increase for a specified period and over the life of the loan.

## CLOSING

The conclusion of a real estate transfer of ownership.

## CLOSING COST

The cost associated with the sale of real estate.

## CONDOMINIUM

A form of real estate ownership. The owner receives a title to specific real estate plus an interest in common areas.

## CREDIT REPORT

A report by a credit reporting agency used by Lenders to determine the credit-worthiness of an applicant.

## CURTESY

The common law interest a husband has in real estate at the time of his wife's death (governed by state law).

## DEED OF TRUST

In some states it is the instrument used in place of a mortgage.

## DEPRECIATION

A loss of value in real estate.

## DISCOUNT/DISCOUNT POINTS/POINTS

In a real estate transaction it is the amount withheld from the loan proceeds by the Lender. This amount is used to adjust the interest rate of the loan to the required yield.

## DOWER

The right of a widow to a life estate in her husband's property at the time of his death (governed by state law).

## DOWN PAYMENT

Cash portion of the amount of the purchase of real estate.

## EARNEST MONEY

The deposit made to a third party by a person purchasing property, held in escrow until the transaction is completed.

## EQUITY

In real estate, it is the difference between the value of the property and the amount owed on the property.

## ESCROW

In some western states, the use of a third party who carries out the wishes of the Buyer and Seller in a real estate closing.

## FANNIE MAE

Federal National Mortgage Association (FNMA).

## FIRST MORTGAGE

A mortgage having priority over all other liens.

## GINNY MAE

Government National Mortgage Association (GNMA).

## HAZARD INSURANCE

An insurance policy where by, for a premium, an insurer agrees to insure property against loss.

## HOMEOWNERS INSURANCE

An insurance policy which covers property and contents.

## HOMESTEAD ESTATE

Owner occupied property is protected by law (up to a certain amount) from attachment and sale for creditor claims (governed by state law).

## IMPOUND

Escrow or reserve payment for items such as taxes, insurance, etc.

## INTEREST RATE

The percentage of an amount of money which is paid for the use of that money over a specified period of time.

## JUDGMENT LIEN

A judgment by the court and placed as a lien against real estate.

## LOAN TO VALUE RATIO

The relationship between the value of property and the loan amount.

## LOSS PAYEE CLAUSE

The clause in an insurance policy indicating who is to be paid in the event of a claim.

## MARGIN

The percentage a Lender adds to the index rate to determine the new interest rate.

## MATURITY

The due date of a note.

## MORTGAGE

The conveyance of interest in real estate used as security for repayment of a note.

## MORTGAGE BANKER

A firm engaging in the field of mortgage banking.

## MORTGAGE BANKING

The packaging of mortgage loans to be sold to a permanent investor. The mortgage banker then retains the servicing of the loan.

## MORTGAGE INSURANCE

Insures the Lender against loss caused by the Borrower's failure to make the payments.

## MORTGAGE NOTE

A written promise to repay a stated amount of money at a stated interest rate over a stated period of time.

## ORIGINATION FEE

A fee charged by a Lender to cover the cost of the process of making a mortgage loan.

## PITI

Principal, Interest, Taxes and Insurance.

## POINTS

See Discount.

## PRINCIPAL

The amount of a debt.

## PRIVATE MORTGAGE INSURANCE (PMI)

See Mortgage Insurance.

## RELEASE OF LIEN

An instrument which discharges a lien.

## RESCISSION

The cancellation of a transaction.

## RESPA

Real Estate Settlement and Procedures Act.

## SECONDARY FINANCING

Any financing on the property **after** a first mortgage.

## SECURITY INSTRUMENT

The mortgage or deed of trust.

## SUBORDINATION

The act of acknowledging that a lien will have a position **after** a mortgage loan. This is accomplished by recording a Subordination Agreement.

## TAX LIEN

A lien against real estate for unpaid taxes.

## TERM

The period of time over which a loan will be repaid.

## TITLE

The evidence of ownership of real property.

## TITLE INSURANCE POLICY

A policy which protects the Lender in the event of a loss due to a defect in the Title. Owner's policy protects the Owner in this same way.

## TRUST DEED

An instrument given by the Borrower to a third party (Trustee) vesting title to the property in the Trustee as security for the Borrower's repayment of the mortgage loan.

## UNDERWRITING

The risk analysis of a Borrower's loan application.

## VACANCY FACTOR

The percentage by which rental income is reduce to cover the anticipated time the property will be vacant.

*SEE THE FOLLOWING PAGES FOR*
*BOOK ORDER FORMS*

Look for all these and other fine Griffin Books
at your favorite bookstore or write to:
# GRIFFIN PUBLISHING

(Please Print)                                        Date _____

Name _____

Address _____

City _____ State _____ Zip _____

Phone ( _____ ) _____

| | PRICE | QTY. | AMOUNT |
|---|---|---|---|
| ***Your Money and Your Home***  Lenz | $12.95 | | |
| ***You're Not Over Drawn —***<br>***Just Underdeposited***  Beverlee Kelley<br>A simple solution to organizing and maintaining<br>control over your finances. | $12.95 | | |
| ***Women: A Guide to the***<br>***Good Old Boys Club***  Judy Johnson<br>This political and women's issues cartoon book<br>is dedicated to women in elected and appointed<br>offices as well as in the workplace. | $7.95 | | |
| ***Harden the Target***  Tom Adams<br>A basic guide to what one should do to reduce<br>their chances of becoming a victim of a violent<br>or property crime. | $10.95 | | |
| ***Worker's Compensation Filing – An***<br>***Employer's Guide to Early Intervention***<br>***and Investigation***  Robert J. Frasco | $49.95 | | |
| | Sub-total | | |
| | CA res. add 8.25% | | |
| | Shipping | | |
| | **TOTAL** | | |

***Shipping:*** 1st book, $1.50
Add'l books, $1.00 each

Check type of payment:

____ Check or money order enclosed

____ Visa  ____ Mastercard

Acct. # _____

Exp. Date _____

Signature _____

Send order to:
**Griffin Publishing
544 W. Colorado St.
Glendale, CA 91204**
Or call to order:
**1-800-423-5789 CA
1-800-826-4849 USA**

Look for all these and other fine Griffin Books
at your favorite bookstore or write to:
# GRIFFIN PUBLISHING

(Please Print)

Date _____

Name _____

Address _____

City _____ State _____ Zip _____

Phone ( _____ ) _____

## *KANTAR ON BRIDGE*

Edward B. Kantar is a world-renowned author on bridge, and winner of many national and international tournaments.

The books available here are not meant for beginners, nor are they aimed at experts. They are directed at players somewhere between these extremes who would like to improve their game substantially. Could this be you?

| | PRICE | QTY. | AMOUNT |
|---|---|---|---|
| *A New Approach to Play and Defense* | $10.95 | | |
| *A Treasury of Bridge Bidding Tips* | $10.95 | | |
| *A Treasury of Bridge Playing Tips* | $10.95 | | |
| | Sub-total | | |
| | CA res. add 8.25% | | |
| | Shipping | | |
| | **TOTAL** | | |

*Shipping:* 1st book, $1.50
2nd book, $1.00 each

Check type of payment:

____ Check or money order enclosed

____ Visa ____ Mastercard

Acct. # _____

Exp. Date _____

Signature _____

Send order to:
**Griffin Publishing
544 W. Colorado St.
Glendale, CA 91204**
Or call to order:
**1-800-423-5789 CA
1-800-826-4849 USA**

Look for all these and other fine Griffin Books
at your favorite bookstore or write to:
## GRIFFIN PUBLISHING

### KANTAR ON BRIDGE

Edward B. Kantar is a world-renowned author on bridge, and winner
of many national and international tournaments.
  The books available here are not meant for beginners, nor are they
aimed at experts. They are directed at players somewhere between
these extremes who would like to improve their game substantially.
Could this be you?

| | PRICE | QTY. | AMOUNT |
|---|---|---|---|
| A New Approach to Play and Defense | $10.95 | | |
| A Treasury of Bridge Bidding Tips | $10.95 | | |
| A Treasury of Bridge Playing Tips | $10.95 | | |
| Sub-total | | | |
| CA res. add 8.25% | | | |
| Shipping | | | |
| TOTAL | | | |

Look for all these and other fine Griffin Books
at your favorite bookstore or write to:
## GRIFFIN PUBLISHING

(Please Print)

Date _____

Name _____

Address _____

City _____ State _____ Zip _____

Phone ( _____ ) _____

| | PRICE | QTY. | AMOUNT |
|---|---|---|---|
| *Your Money and Your Home*  Lenz | $12.95 | | |
| *You're Not Over Drawn —*<br>*Just Underdeposited*  Beverlee Kelley<br>A simple solution to organizing and maintaining<br>control over your finances. | $12.95 | | |
| *Women: A Guide to the*<br>*Good Old Boys Club*  Judy Johnson<br>This political and women's issues cartoon book<br>is dedicated to women in elected and appointed<br>offices as well as in the workplace. | $7.95 | | |
| *Harden the Target*  Tom Adams<br>A basic guide to what one should do to reduce<br>their chances of becoming a victim of a violent<br>or property crime. | $10.95 | | |
| *Worker's Compensation Filing – An*<br>*Employer's Guide to Early Intervention*<br>*and Investigation*  Robert J. Frasco | $49.95 | | |
| | Sub-total | | |
| | CA res. add 8.25% | | |
| | Shipping | | |
| | **TOTAL** | | |

*Shipping:* 1st book, $1.50
Add'l books, $1.00 each

Check type of payment:

___ Check or money order enclosed

___ Visa  ___ Mastercard

Acct. # _____

Exp. Date _____

Signature _____

Send order to:
**Griffin Publishing**
**544 W. Colorado St.**
**Glendale, CA 91204**
Or call to order:
**1-800-423-5789 CA**
**1-800-826-4849 USA**